AF352454

THE CATHOLIC UNIVERSITY OF AMERICA
CANON LAW STUDIES
No. 98

# THE PENAL LAW FOR RELIGIOUS

## A DISSERTATION

*Submitted to the Faculty of Canon Law of the
Catholic University of America in Partial
Fulfillment of the Requirements for
the Degree of*

### DOCTOR OF CANON LAW

BY THE

REVEREND MARINER THEODORE SMITH, O.P., S.T.Lr., J.C.L.
Of the Province of Saint Joseph

THE CATHOLIC UNIVERSITY OF AMERICA
WASHINGTON, D. C.
1935

C O N T E N T S

**PAGE**

FOREWORD ................................................................................ vii

**PART I**

**HISTORICAL DEVELOPMENT OF THE PENAL LAW
FOR RELIGIOUS**

INTRODUCTION TO THE HISTORICAL STUDY ............. ix

**CHAPTER I**

**THE ANCIENT LAW AND THE DECREE OF GRATIAN**.... 3

**CHAPTER II**

**FROM THE DECREE OF GRATIAN TO THE DECRETALS** 14

**CHAPTER III**

**FROM THE DECRETALS TO THE COUNCIL OF TRENT** 21

**CHAPTER IV**

**FROM THE COUNCIL OF TRENT TO THE CODE**........... 25

**PART II**

**COMMENTARY ON THE PRESENT LAW**

**SECTION I**

**OFFENSES AGAINST THE GENERAL LAWS OF THE
CHURCH**

**CHAPTER I**

AGAINST THE FAITH ITSELF................................................ 39

   ARTICLE 1. APOSTASY.  CANON 646, § 1, N. 1° ............ 39

   ARTICLE 2. *Ipso Jure* DISMISSAL.  CANON 646 ............ 47



iii

## CHAPTER II


PAGE

AGAINST ECCLESIASTICAL AUTHORITY .......................... 51

    ARTICLE 1. AGAINST THE AUTHORITY OF SUPERIORS. CANON 2331, § 2 ......................... 51

    ARTICLE 2. AGAINST THE AUTHORITY AND RIGHTS OF THE CHURCH. CANON 2331, § 1 ......................... 54

        § 1. Issuing Laws, Decrees, etc., Against the Rights and Liberties of the Church. Canon 2334, § 1 ......................... 54

        § 2. Impeding the Exercise of Ecclesiastical Jurisdiction By Recourse to Lay Power. Canon 2334, § 2 ......................... 56

    ARTICLE 3. ENROLLMENT IN MASONIC SECTS AND SIMILAR ASSOCIATIONS. CANON 2335 ......................... 58


## CHAPTER III


VIOLATION OF THE CLOISTER ......................... 64

    ARTICLE 1. CLOISTER OF MALE REGULARS. CANON 2342, N. 2° ......................... 64

    ARTICLE 2. CLOISTER OF NUNS. CANON 2342, N. 3° ......................... 72


## CHAPTER IV


FORGERY AND FALSIFICATION OF DOCUMENTS OF THE HOLY SEE. CANON 2360 ......................... 76


## CHAPTER V


CONTUMACIOUS NEGLECT OF DIOCESAN CONFERENCES. CANON 2337 ......................... 81


## CHAPTER VI


COMMERCIAL TRADING. CANON 2380 ......................... 84

## CHAPTER VII

PAGE

### PENALTIES AGAINST DISMISSED RELIGIOUS CLERICS.

Canons 648, 669, § 2; 670, 671 ............ 87

## SECTION II

## CRIMES AGAINST THE RELIGIOUS STATE

## CHAPTER VIII

### UNLAWFUL DEPARTURE FROM RELIGION

UNLAWFUL DEPARTURE FROM RELIGION............ ........ 94

Article 1. Apostasy from Religion. Canon 2385 ........ 94

Article 2. Fugitives. Canon 2386 ............ 100

Article 3. Flight with Person of Opposite Sex. Canon 646, § 1, n. 1° ............ 104

## CHAPTER IX

### PROFESSION INVALIDATED BY FRAUD. Canon 2387.

PROFESSION INVALIDATED BY FRAUD. Canon 2387.. 108

## CHAPTER X

### SACRILEGIOUS MARRIAGE

SACRILEGIOUS MARRIAGE ............ 111

Article 1. Attempted By Solemnly Professed Regulars. Canon 2388, § 1 ............ 111

Article 2. Attempted or Contracted By Religious with Simple Perpetual Vows. Canon 2388, § 2 ............ 117

Article 3. Attempted or Contracted By Any Religious ............ 119

§ 1. *Ipso Jure* Dismissal. Canon 646, § 1, n. 3° ............ 119

§ 2. Irregularity. Canon 985, n. 3° ............ 120

## CHAPTER XI

PAGE

VIOLATION OF THE COMMON LIFE.  CANON 2389 ........ 124

### SECTION III

ABUSE OF POWER BY RELIGIOUS SUPERIORS
IN GENERAL

## CHAPTER XII

REGARDING THE ORDINATION OF RELIGIOUS.
CANON 2410 ........................ 128

## CHAPTER XIII

REGARDING ADMISSION OF CANDIDATES TO NOVI-
TIATE AND PROFESSION.  CANON 2411 ........ 132

## CHAPTER XIV

INTERFERENCE WITH CANONICAL VISITATION.
CANON 2413 ........................ 139

### SECTION IV

ABUSE OF POWER BY SUPERIORESS IN PARTICULAR

## CHAPTER XV

REGARDING DOWRIES AND NOTIFICATION TO LOCAL
ORDINARY OF RECEPTION OR PROFESSION.  CANON
2412 ........................ 144

    ARTICLE 1. DOWRIES ........................ 144

    ARTICLE 2. NOTIFICATION TO LOCAL ORDINARY OF RECEP-
TION AND PROFESSION ........................ 146

## CHAPTER XVI

INTERFERENCE WITH THE LIBERTY OF CONFES-
SION. CANON 2414 ........................ 149

BIBLIOGRAPHY ........................ 154

ALPHABETICAL INDEX ........................ 161

# THE PENAL LAW FOR RELIGIOUS

## FOREWORD

In this study we shall consider the Penal Law for Religious as it stands in the Common Law of the Church, excluding altogether any particular laws of orders, congregations or localities and confining ourselves solely to the General Law of the Latin Church. Furthermore we must exclude all laws which affect religious only in common with others of the faithful, unless there be a special added sanction applicable to religious as such. Lastly we shall not consider any laws which incidentally affect religious but only under some other aspect, such, for instance, as a local ordinary or a parish priest, or as clerics "whether secular or religious." We must include, however, any law that affects only a certain general class of religious, as for example, clerical religious, regulars, nuns, because it is as religious, even though a somewhat specific class of religious, that they are affected.

There is not, and never has been, what could properly be called a Penal Code of, or for, Religious. The Code itself contains a Title (Bk. V, Tit. XVII), on "Delicts against the Obligations Proper to the Clerical or Religious State," but as is evident from its title it is not exclusively concerned with religious, nor are more than six of our canons taken from this title, while five others, those of the last two headings dealing with abuse of power, are taken from the XIX Title of the Fifth Book, on "Abuse of Power of Ecclesiastical Office."

Though the organization of this particular phase of the law seems somewhat unsatisfactory, it is nevertheless, an immense step forward from the pre-Code law. As late a work as the renowned *Jus Decretalium* of Wernz (Prato edition, 1913), contains no Section, Title or Chapter on this subject, though the entire second Section of the third Book of his sixth Volume deals with Offenses Proper to Clerics.

The author takes this occasion to express his gratitude and appreciation to all who have assisted in the production of this work, and in particular to the members of the Canon Law Faculty and to those friends and members of his own Order, without whose aid its composition would have been impossible.

vii

# PART I

HISTORICAL DEVELOPMENT OF THE PENAL
LAW FOR RELIGIOUS

# INTRODUCTION TO PART I

The history of this subject naturally reaches back almost, but not quite as far as the history of religious life itself. It does not reach back quite as far as the beginning of religious life, because it is an almost universal rule that great idealistic movements, which have their inception in the loftiest ideals and noblest sentiments of the human heart, are at first, and in their first protagonists, free from those disorders which require a penal law. It is only with time that abuses creep in, fervor relaxes, idealism wanes, and offenses commence which shortly can only be met by penalties and the growth of a penal law. At first, too, penal law, like all law, is quite simple and glaring, and though the penalties are few they are severe. So it is that in the earliest stage of the law in hand we find two principal offenses, severely punished by law—Desertion and Infidelity. Those who abandoned the religious state and those who were unfaithful to their vow of chastity were punished with the utmost rigor—reduction to military servitude, confiscation of goods, and excommunication.

But to trace the development of this particular phase of penal law it seems best to divide the field chronologically and note the development of the subject by periods. The first period would cover the time up to and including Gratian's compilation. The second period would extend from Gratian (1150) to the Decretals of Gregory IX (1234) with the appendixed Sixth Book of Boniface VIII (1298) and the Clementines of Clement V (1317). The third period would extend from the Clementines to the Council of Trent (1563), and the fourth from Trent to the Code (1918).

# CHAPTER I

## FIRST PERIOD

### THE ANCIENT LAW AND DECREE OF GRATIAN

THE "Decree of Gratian" is the first monumental work in the
*Corpus Juris Canonici.* While it never became a public official collection [1] it stands chronologically at the head of the *Corpus* and from
its antiquity has obtained universal recognition. However, it is not
a source of law in itself, but simply a collection of already existing
laws which merely retain *per se* the authority they had in themselves.
Moreover, though they gained nothing legally from inclusion in this
collection, in fact these excerpts taken from local councils, ecclesiastical writers, and even civil laws, did now become at least to some
extent the general jurisprudence of the universal Church, and it is
this fact alone which justifies our dealing with what were originally,
in many cases, merely local laws.

It is generally agreed that organized religious life arose about
the middle of the third century of our era, having as its immediate
progenitors the ascetics of the Egyptian desert and the orders of
virgins in the West, especially in Rome.[2] Their organization had not
attained a definite maturity long before the first Ecumenical Council, Nicea, held in 325 under Pope St. Sylvester I and the Emperor
Constantine the Great. In the Acts of this Council is found the
first general legislation regarding religious and likewise the first
penal legislation in their regard. Added to the Acts of the Council
is a special supplement entitled, "Decrees and Constitutions Concerning Monks and Anchorites," and the last chapter of this supplement
is a chapter entitled, "Delicts and Penalties of Monks."[3] The legis-

---

[1] Cicognani, H. J., *Canon Law* (Philadelphia, 1934), p. 287 ff.

[2] *Cf.* Schäfer, T., De *Religiosis* (Munster, 1927), pp. 10-12; Wernz, F. X.,
*Jus Decretalium,* Vol. IV (Prato, 1913), p. 530 ff; Steiger, J., "De Vitae Reli-
giosae Propagationes et Diffusione Synopsis Historica," in *Periodica de Re
Canonica,* Vol. XIII (Rome, 1924), p. 36 ff.

[3] Mansi, J. D., *Collectio Amplissima SS. Conciliorum,* 2, 1018. Hefele
(English translation, Vol. I, p. 363ff.) proves these constitutions spurious.

lation of this chapter is very general. It merely states that a monk guilty of a crime is to be punished by his superiors, and if he does not amend, separated from the company of the faithful. If even this does not suffice he is to be excommunicated publicly. This entire supplement is certainly unauthentic.

However, this does not exhaust the Council's enactments on this matter. Canon 3 had struck strongly at the *"virgines subintroductae"* [4] and Canon 16 pronounces deposition and privation of their ministry against any monk engaging in money-lending, usury, or other illicit means of enrichment.[5] Finally in Chapter XLIII the Council decrees that if a monk or cleric falls into any sin, and being called on three times by the Congregation, does not purge himself, he is to be expelled and degraded.[6]

Thus stood the law after the first Ecumenical Council. The second, at Constantinople (381), and the third, that of Ephesus (431), enacted no new penal legislation against religious. Neither are there any papal laws on the matter. It is well to remark here that when dealing with papal pronouncements at this time it is almost impossible to determine whether the Pope is promulgating a law, giving advice or direction in a particular case, or simply making remarks about conditions. Hence, it is best to deal with the papal regulations when found in a body of laws, that is, the Decree of Gratian.

The Fourth Ecumenical Council, Chalcedon (451), added to the meager store of penal law for religious. By this time the cenobitical life was very fully developed, the Rules of St. Pachomius, St. Basil and St. Augustine were already being followed by numerous com-

---

[4] These *"virgines subintroductae"* were an institution that had sprung up in the third century, before the organization of community life. Consecrated virgins and men vowed to celibacy contracted "spiritual marriages" and lived together "as brother and sister." The practice became fairly widespread in the fourth century but, from its nature dangerous, it was combated and finally suppressed by ecclesiastical authorities. It is only just to remark that few if any authentic records of actual abuse among Catholics have come down to us and probably most cases remained free from corruption. The advent of community life took away the conditions that gave rise to this queer institution. *Cf.* Steiger, *op cit.*, p. 42 ff. Hefele, *Histoire des Conciles*, Vol. I, p. 538.

[5] Mansi, 2, 986; Hardouin, 1, 330.

[6] Mansi, 2, 966, unauthentic supplement. *Cf.* supra note 3.

munities, and in less than half a century more St. Benedict was to launch the great organization of Western monasticism, the Benedictine Order.

With maturity comes the beginning of decay, and while the various communities and rules doubtless had each their own more or less definite penal laws, the Council of Chalcedon found it necessary to take some matters into its own hands, which it proceeded to do in one chapter and three canons.

In the first of these, Chapter III, the Council decrees that monks or clerics who gather possessions or mix in secular business unless perhaps to care for minors, widows and orphans, shall be subject to ecclesiastical punishment.[7]  Taken from Chapter VI of the First Council of Carthage (348) [8] it was incorporated into the Decree of Gratian and is cited amongst the sources of Canon 2380 of the Code, which contains the penalty against clerics and religious engaging in commercial enterprises.  The Council, however, adds no further penalty for religious than for other clerics.

The next penalty is contained in Canon 3, which anathematizes monks or clerics who leave to join the army or pursue secular honors.[9] This canon, likewise, included in Gratian, is one of the sources of Canon 2385 of the Code, the one which deals with apostates from religion.  Canon 16, cited amongst the sources for Canon 2388 of the Code, pronounces excommunication against monks and virgins who marry, while authorizing bishops to show mercy,[10] and Canon 18, a source of our Canon 2336, § 1, decrees that monks who shall be found plotting or conspiring against bishops or clergy are to be altogether deposed from their own rank.[11]

---

[7] Mansi, 7, 373 and 374; apud Gratianum, c. 26, D. LXXXVI; Hardouin, 2, 601; Berardi, 1, 233.

[8] Mansi, 3, 147; Hardouin, 1, 686; apud Gratianum, c. 1, C. XXI, q. 3; Berardi, 1, 233.

[9] Mansi, 7, 375; Hardouin, 2, 603; apud Gratianum, c. 3, C. XX, q. 3; Berardi, 1-2, 273.

[10] Mansi, 7, 377, 378; Hardouin, 2, 607; apud Gratianum, c. 22, C. XXVII, q. 1; Berardi, 1, 241.

[11] Mansi, 7, 378; Hardouin, 2, 609; apud Gratianum, c. 23, C. XI, q. 1; Berardi, 1, 235.

The next four General Councils, Second, Third and Fourth of Constantinople and the Second of Nicea added nothing to the penal law of religious, and the Council in Trullo, or *Quinisexti,* which did make a gesture or two in that direction never was recognized as an ecumenical council, and therefore, its legislation had not universal binding force.  All these councils were overwhelmingly oriental in personnel and in interests, and consequently, contributed little to development of Western discipline.

Meanwhile, however, there were contributions from Roman Law, especially from the Code and the Novels of Justinian.  The Code prescribes that those who leave the monastery and return to the world forfeit all their property to the monastery.[12]  His fifth novel restates this law and adds further that these deserters are to be attached to the military service of the Governor of the Province.[13]  His one hundred and twenty-third novel threatens with capital punishment anyone who violates a nun or any woman wearing a religious habit, together with all the participants in the crime, and commands the woman if she be guilty to be kept more securely in the monastery lest she fall again.[14]

It is interesting to note the difference between the punishment in Justinian's law for unchastity on the part of nuns and on the part of deaconesses.  The former seems to be merely a sort of imprisonment in the monastery, while the latter make themselves liable to capital punishment.[15]  Still, since Novel 123 was promulgated nine years after the one prescribing death for unchaste deaconesses, and it mentions deaconesses as well as simple nuns, it seems to have changed the former law and abolished the death penalty against deaconesses.

For more than two centuries and a half after Second Nicea no ecumenical council was held in the Church.  Meanwhile Europe, the Church and the Papacy had gone through the Iron Age carrying monasticism with them to share their vicissitudes.  The Great Schism

---

[12] *Cod.* 1, 3, 54, 7.

[13] *Corpus Juris Civilis, Nov. Justiniani,* 5, cap. 6, *de Monachis.*

[14] *C. J. C., Nov. Just.,* 123, Cap. 43; *apud Gratianum,* c. 30, C. XXVII, q. 1; Berardi, 3, 381.

[15] *C. J. C., Nov. Just.,* 6, Cap. 6.

had broken off the Oriental Church, the Cluniac reform of monasticism and the Hildebrandine reform of the Church had taken strong root, and Pope St. Gregory VII had already died in the battle for reform when the next General Council, the First Lateran, met in 1123, under Pope Callistus II, to terminate the warfare with the Holy Roman Emperors. The principal objects of the reformers' attacks had been clerical concubinage and lay investiture. Hence legislation touching on these and surrounding points was to be expected. In this particular phase of law, however, very little indeed was forthcoming. Canon 21 forbids clerics in major orders, and monks, to have concubines, and commands that if any of them have contracted marriage they are to be separated and "return to penance according to the definition of the canons." [16] Gratian quotes it attributing it to a Council of Rheims under Urban II, and it is listed among the sources of Canon 2388. As is evident it is most indeterminate and in no sense applies exclusively to religious. Moreover it is the only bit of penal legislation against religious passed by the Council. There is doubtless a twofold reason for this. One is that the Cluniac reform had so revivified monastic life that such legislation was not necessary at that particular time; the other is that the Benedictine Rule, then the basic law of all Latin Religious Institutes, contained in itself a sufficient penal code.[17]

The next General Council, Second Lateran, under Innocent II, followed after a lapse of but sixteen years (1139). Restating in Canon 7 the law of First Lateran quoted above in slightly different words by prescribing "condign penance" for offenders, Canon 8 extends the law with its penalty to nuns likewise if they attempt to marry.[18] These canons incorporated by Gratian are likewise cited as sources for Canon 2388 of the Code.

The very next Canon of Second Lateran, however, not found in Gratian or cited amongst the Fontes of the Code is taken from Canon

[16] Mansi, 21, 286; Hardouin, 6b, 1114; apud Gratianum, c. 8, D. XXVII; Berardi, 1, 443.

[17] *Regula Sti Benedicti*, Cap. II, III, XXIII-XXIX, XXXII, XXXIII, XLII-XLIV, XLVIII, LI, LIV, LV, LXII, LXV, LXVII, LXIX-LXXI.

[18] Mansi, 21, 527, 528; Hardouin, 6b, 1209; apud Gratianum, c. 40, C. XXVII, q. 1.

6 of the Council of Rheims held earlier under the same Pontiff, and
forbids monks and canons regular to learn laws or medicine in order
to make money. The penalty, spoilation of the superiors' own honors,
is fulminated against the bishops, abbots and priors who permit their
subjects to learn these things.[19] This law seems to have given rise
shortly to kindred enactments as shall be seen later on in the law of
Alexander III in the Council of Tours, and a later one of Honorius
III, both found in the Decretals. These later laws lost sight of the
main point of the Lateran Canon, the final clause, *i. e.*, "to make
money," and simply forbade the study of laws, etc. As stated here
the canon bears a direct relationship to Canon 2380 of the Code.

This was the tenth and last ecumenical council before Gratian
compiled his Decree, and it was this meager bit of legislation that
made up the certainly official penal law for religious at that time.
There were a great many papal pronouncements on the matter, but
their force was in many, if not most cases, uncertain. It was from
these, together with the writings of the fathers and the decrees of
particular councils that Gratian made his collection.

As might be expected, one of the earliest papal letters in our
field quoted by Gratian deals with apostates. It is one attributed
to St. Leo the Great addressed to Rusticus, a bishop. In it he declares that any monk who leaves his profession (religious life) and
embraces the military or married life is to be "purged by the satisfaction of public penance." [20]

Next in line of antiquity comes Pope St. Innocent I's letter to
Victricius, Bishop of Rouen. In it he decrees that a solemnly
veiled virgin who marries or is corrupted cannot be admitted to
penance unless her accomplice "retires from the world" (*de saeculo
recesserit*). This sounds rather severe, but the context makes it
much more so. The conclusion seems almost inescapable that "retires from the world" means not merely "till he enters a monastery"
but "until he dies," for the Pope cites and applies the case of a

---

[19] Mansi, 21, 528; Migne, P. L., 179, 680; Conc. Lat., II, Canon 9, Hardouin,
6b, 1209.

[20] St. Leo I, *Ep.* (XC, Vol. XCII) *ad Rusticum;* apud Gratianum, c. 1, C.
XX, q. 3. Cannot verify it in Mansi or Migne.

married woman who joins herself to another man, and being an adulteress is not admitted to penance unless one of them shall have died (*nisi unus ex eis defunctus fuerit*). The virgin who is not veiled and breaks her promise of virginity is to be subjected to penance for some time, but escapes the severity of the punishment against the consecrated.[21]

Pope St. Gregory the Great reiterates this law of Innocent, applies it also to widows, and condemns these latter to imprisonment as well, after they have been separated, willingly or unwillingly, from the man.[22]

Gregory in his several letters deals with this question many times. In a letter to a certain Cyprian he merely states that a violated nun and her corruptor are to be punished [23] but in a letter to John, Bishop of Cagliara, he prescribes "severe canonical penalties," followed by confinement in a stricter monastery and the practice of severer fasts and austerities for any nun who shall fall into adultery.[24] While in another place he directs a bishop to bring back and enclose in the monastery a consecrated woman now living in concubinage.[25] This certainly seems to be a particular instruction for an individual case, but Gratian has incorporated it in his Decree. Of a like nature are Canons 18 and 19 of this same Cause where he instructs Vitalian, the Bishop of Sipontinus (now Manfredonia), and the Civil Magistrate Sergius to bring back by force and imprison in her monastery a cer-

---

[21] Mansi, 3, 1035; Migne, P. L., 21, 478-480. Innocentius I, *Epist. II ad Victricium*, Ep. Cop. 13 and 14; apud Gratianum, c. 9, 10, C. XXVII, q. 1. Several mss. have *"discesserit"* (departs) instead of *"recesserit"* (retires).

[22] St. Gregory the Great, *ep. ad. Bonifatium ep.;* apud Gratianum, c. 2, C. XXVII, q. 1. Note that the Second Leipsig Edition states that this is the title given in all collections, but the substance is found in the Capitularies, Cap. 215. It does not form part of the letter to Boniface given as Ep. V, Lib. IV, apud Migne, P. L., 77, 672; apud Gratianum, c. 9, D. XXXII.

[23] Migne, P. L., 77, 672, 673; Gregorius I, *Ad Cyprianum*, Lib. IV, Ep. VI.

[24] St. Gregory the Great to John, *Ep of Cagliara*, Lib. III, Ep. IX; apud Gratianum, c. 28, C. XXVII, q. 1. Not given in Liber III, Ep. IX, in Migne, P. L., 77, 612, where letter is *"ad Antonium."*

[25] C. 15, C. XXVII, q. 1. Attributed to Gregory, but not recognizable in his works (footnote).

tain apostate nun, the daughter of Tullian.[26]   Finally, in a letter to
Artemius or Anthemius, a Subdeacon, he commands the latter to
search out all wandering and married monks and by coercion, if necessary, force them to return to their monasteries.[27]

These instructions and decrees of the great monk-pope are found
today amongst the sources of Canons 2385 and 2388 of the Code.

Pope St. Nicholas I in a letter to Albinus, Archbishop of Vienna,
cites a new type of ecclesiastical offender, namely, women who pretended to be nuns, adopted a religious habit, etc., and then, when the
opportunity offered, abandoned it or married.   He decrees that,
"unless they come to their senses" (*nisi resipiscant*), they shall be
struck with the spiritual sword.[28]   The thought seems to be that they
shall be considered bound to the obligations of that state which they
pretended to have embraced, as a penalty for their fraud.

Before passing from papal legislation to that of particular councils
we should note an alleged decree of Pope St. Eutychian, martyr, who
reigned from 275 to 283.   It condemns to canonical judgment until
satisfaction is given, any abbess or nun who thereafter has the
audacity to give the veil to any widow or young virgin.[29]   The at-
tribution of this decree to St. Eutychian is obviously erroneous as
the beginnings of religious life had not been organized in his
pontificate.   It is doubtless a late conciliar decree of Paris.

As remarked in the beginning, almost all the early penalties
against religious were aimed against those who deserted or those who
violated their vow of chastity.   Nowhere is this more strikingly
brought out than in the conciliar legislation incorporated into the
Decree of Gratian.   All but one of these synodal laws deal with either
apostasy or unchastity.

First, let us take those dealing with desertion or apostasy, and
for the sake of greater convenience follow the order in Gratian.

---

[26] C. 18, 19, C. XXVII, q. 1 (Greg. to Vitalian, Lib. VII, Indict. 1, epis. 9
and 10).

[27] Migne, P. L., 77, 495; Lib. I, Ep. 42; apud Gratianum, c. 39, C. XXVII,
q. 1.

[28] Nicholas I ad Albinum Abp. Vienn., apud Gratianum, c. 6, 7, D. XXVII.

[29] C. 3, C. XX, q. 2, *Ep. Eutyciani Papae.*   Footnote in Leipsig II cites it
from c. 43, liber I, Conc. Paris VI; Mansi, 14, 564.

The first of these laws comes from the Second Council of Arles and prescribes that those who have apostatized from religion shall not receive Communion until they have done penance. Furthermore, they shall not be admitted to the clerical office and if, after penance, they relapse again and resume the secular habit, they shall be held "alien from the Church," *i. e.,* excommunicated.[80]

The Sixth Council of Toledo also decrees that men or women once clothed with the habit are to be forced to return to it if they desert and if they will not return they are to be excommunicated. Widows who desert are to be condemned by the sentence of the superior.[31]

The First Council of Orleans, in the same vein, punishes with separation from the company of the faithful and from the reception of Communion, anyone who after penance leaves religion and returns to the world, and it strengthens this punishment by depriving of Communion anyone who eats with the apostate after the interdict.[32] All these are among the sources of Canon 2385 of the present Code of Canon Law.

There are more conciliar enactments against unchastity than there were against apostates. Even before Chalcedon a Council of Carthage had pronounced excommunication against widows who, having made a vow of chastity and put on a religious habit, left and married.[33] The Fourth Council of Toledo (633) suspends from Communion until they amend, girls and widows who marry despite vows [34] and also commands that all monks who left their monastery and not only returned to the world, but took wives as well, be brought back to the monastery and there subjected to penance "and there

[80] Mansi, 7, 881, Conc. Arles II, Cap. 25; Hardouin, 2, 755; apud Gratianum, c. 29, D. L.

[31] Mansi, 10, 665, Conc. Toletano VI, Canon 6; Hardouin, 3, 604; apud Gratianum, c. 2, C. XX.

[32] Mansi, 8, 353 and 354, Conc. Aurelianensi I, c. 13; Hardouin, 2, 1008; Hefele, 2, 1012; apud Gratianum, c. 5, C. XXXIII, q. 3; D. V., *de Poenit.*

[33] Mansi, 3, 959, Conc. Carthage I, c. 104; apud Gratianum, c. 1, C. XXVII, q. 1. Better cited from the *Statuta Ecclesiae Antiquae—ibid.*

[34] Mansi, 10, 629, Conc. Toletano IV, Canon 8; apud Gratianum, c. 7, C. XXVII, q. 1.

amend where they had failed." [35]   The girls and widows are to be
perpetually excluded from Communion and the society of the faithful if they do not amend.

The Council of Tribur (695) enacted an important canon on this
subject which was incorporated into the Decree as four canons.   It
pronounced against monks, nuns and consecrated virgins who marry
and procreate children the sentence of expulsion from the monastery,
life imprisonment, excommunication, and only allowed them Viaticum
"by a consideration of mercy."   Furthermore, those who marry nuns
are to be separated from them and do penance for life, while those
who commit sacrilege with consecrated virgins are to be deprived
of Communion and never admitted to It again, unless they perform
public penance.   However, if they repent worthily they are not to be
denied Viaticum. [36]

The Fifth Council of Orleans reiterates the decrees of Chalcedon
and Tribur and merely adds the command that all consecrated women
who have married be separated from their husbands. [37]

The most terrible penalty of all is that of the Council of Elvira
(305), which "ordered that virgins who have dedicated themselves to
God, if they shall lose (or betray) the pact of virginity and gratify
their lust, not understanding what they are giving up, are not to be
given Communion even at the end (of life).   But if they have fallen
once, led astray by the weakness of the body, and for the whole
period of their life, done penance and abstained from coition, it orders
that they ought to receive Communion at the end." [38]   This canon, it
is true, was not the law of the Roman Church, but of a Plenary or
National Spanish Council of the earliest times.   Nevertheless, it was
not purely local to Spain for the third Council of Mainz (888) quotes
and adopts this Canon of Elvira in its own Canon 26, [39] almost six

[35] Mansi, 10, 631 and 632, Conc. Toletano IV, Canon 52; Hardouin, 3, 589.

[36] Mansi, 18ᵃ, 148, Conc. Tribur, Canon 6; apud Gratianum, cc. 11, 12, 13, 14,
C. XXVII, q. 1.

[37] Mansi, 9, 129, Conc. Aurelianensi V, c. e.; apud Gratianum, c. 16, C.
XXVII, q. 1.

[38] Mansi, 2, 8, Council of Elvira, Canon 13; Hardouin, 1, 251; apud Gratianum, c. 25, C. XXVII, q. 1.

[39] Mansi, 18ᵃ, 73 and 74, Conc. Moguntino, Cap. 26; Hardouin 6ᵃ, 410.

centuries after its promulgation in Spain, and a Cologne Council repeats it still later. It is impossible to discover what force was added to it by inclusion in Gratian's Decree, and when it fell into disuse.

All these laws, with the Canon taken from the first Council of Orleans, which bars monks who marry from ever obtaining any ecclesiastical rank [40] are amongst the sources of Canon 2388 of the 1918 Code, most, though not all of them being cited as such in the footnotes of the Gasparri edition.

There is only one other Canon of Gratian among our sources, the one cited in the note to Canon 2389, regarding common life. It merely quotes St. Augustine's Rule where he ordains the condemnation of a thief to be passed against those who violate the common life.[41]

This completes the sketch of the Penal Law of Religious in the "Ancient Law" and in Gratian, the first nine centuries of organized monasticism, and brings to an end the First Period.

[40] Mansi, 8, 355, Conc. Aurelian I, cc. 22 and 23; Hardouin, 2, 1410; apud Gratianum, c. 30, C. XXVII, q. 1.

[41] Migne, P. L., 32, 1377-1384, 211 Letter of St. Augustine; apud Gratianum, c. 11, C. XII, q. 1.

## CHAPTER II

## SECOND PERIOD

### UNDER THE DECREE AND THE DECRETALS

The century between the Decree of Gratian and the Decretals of Gregory IX was a very short time in comparison with the first period of nine centuries, but it was a very full and very momentous time in the development of Canon Law and of religious life. Two very important ecumenical councils were held during this period, Third and Fourth Lateran under Alexander III and Innocent III, respectively, themselves brilliant canonists. Likewise, during this period the religious life broke away from its stable monastic moorings and developed into new forms: the Military Orders, founded just before the period begins; the orders for the redemption of captives, and the Mendicant Friars. With the loss of the bulwark of enclosure and stability the religious found themselves in more perilous circumstances; the result was an increase in accidents and a consequent increase in penal laws.

As was the case with the papal documents in Gratian's Decree, so too in the Decretals it is frequently impossible to discern which were laws of universal binding force in the beginning, and which were merely particular responses or individual counsel. But there is this great difference; while inclusion in Gratian's Decree gave no law any greater binding force than it had in the beginning, promulgation in the Decretals made it henceforth a law of Gregory IX, binding everywhere no matter what its source may have been. Therefore, the laws will be taken in the order in which they appear in the Decretals, regardless of their chronological order, except, as in the case of a conciliar decree, where it is patent that the law has been universal from the beginning.

The Third Lateran Council (1179) devotes its tenth chapter to penal legislation for monks, particularly as regards simony and offenses against the common life. It forbids the reception of monks for a price and interdicts the promotion to sacred orders of anyone who

14

has given anything, even though demanded, for his reception, and it inflicts privation of office on anyone who accepts such gift. It further goes on to suspend from Communion anyone in illegitimate possession of private money (*peculium*) and decrees that anyone found in possession of it at death shall not be buried "amongst the brethren," nor shall offering be made for him. Abbots are commanded under pain of privation of office to take diligent care of this matter, and if the priorate or any obedience is given to anyone for a price both giver and receiver become "alien from ecclesiastical ministry." [1]

First in order is an instruction of Pope Innocent III to a certain Archbishop Ausitanus in which he complains of the disordered state of monks, canons, and other regulars in this prelate's province where abuses in regard to enclosure, money, the common life and obedience in general are rampant. He directs the Archbishop to warn these erring regulars to return to their monastery, give their possessions to their prelates for the use of the house, and observe the regular life. If their prelates, after this warning, neglect to execute it they are to be compelled to do so by suspension from office and benefice, without any appeal.[2] This was given at the Lateran, March 17, 1198, and is, as is also the above chapter of Third Lateran, a source for Canon 2389 of the Code.

The only other contribution from the First Book of the Decretals is cited among the sources of Canon 2385 on apostates and is taken from an instruction of Alexander III to a Spanish Bishop and the Prior of St. Mary of Saragossa. The rubric in the Decretals merely states that one professed in religion under fear of death may, if he has not later ratified the profession, leave and marry, but not if he has freely consented either from the beginning or later. Alexander's instruction says that if one has entered freely or later ratified his profession, he is to be compelled by ecclesiastical censure to return to his monastery and resume his habit should he leave.[3]

From the Second Book comes a response of Innocent III to the

---

[1] Conc. Lat. III, Cap. 10, c. 2, X, *de statu monachorum et canonicorum regularium*, III, 35; Mansi, 21, 225.

[2] C. 7, X, *de officio judicis ordinarii*, I, 31.

[3] C. 1, X, *de his quae vi metusve causa fiunt*, I, 40.

Bishop of Imola exposing certain religious superiors who claimed to have letters and indults from the Pope exempting them altogether from the subjection to the bishop regarding priories. He directs that they be punished as guilty of forgery.[4]  Though not cited in the sources, it bears relation to Canon 2360 on the Crime of Forgery.

In the Third Book there is much more to the point, and first of all is a law of Gregory IX himself.  He commands religious superiors to seek annually for all their dismissed or fugitive subjects, and to receive them back, if their order permits, under pain of censure.  If this is not permissible, they shall be consigned for penance to other religious houses, preferably other monasteries of the same order. But if these fugitives or dismissed shall be found disobedient, they are to be excommunicated and publicly denounced as such by the prelates of the churches, until they humbly return.[5]  This is a source of Canon 2386, concerning fugitive religious, but it is stricter than the present law which carries only a suspension of those in sacred orders and loss of exemption by those who enjoy it, instead of the excommunication laid down here.

The next pertinent chapter restates the law of Third Lateran treated above about simony and peculium [6] and is followed by an instruction of Clement III recalling that law and interpreting "burial among the brethren" of which the guilty ones were to be deprived, as Christian burial, and he further directs that if one of them has been buried in consecrated ground the corpse is to be ejected therefrom if it can be done without scandal.[7]

Innocent III, in a decree of 1202 addressed to the Abbot of Subiaco, touching on the same point, decrees dismissal, without hope of readmittance unless they repent, of any guilty of this abuse, and if they die in the vice of property they shall be buried in a dump (*sterquilino*) outside the monastery.[8]

The next pertinent chapter contains a strange and severe law.

---

[4] C. 6, X, *de confimatione utili vel inutili*, II, 30.

[5] C. 24, X, *de regularibus et transeuntibus ad religionem*, III, 31.

[6] Conc. Lat. III, Cap. 10, c. 2, X, *de statu monachorum et canonicorum regularium*, III, 35.

[7] C. 4, *ex eodem titulo.*

[8] C. 6, *ex eodem titulo.*

It will be recalled that the Second Lateran Council forbade monks to study laws and medicine *to make money,*[9] the idea being to stop an abuse against monastic poverty.  Here Alexander III, in the Council of Tours, forbids under pain of excommunication, any professed religious to study physics or "mundane" laws, and giving those engaged in such studies two months to return to their monasteries, prescribing further that, if they do not return within that time, when they return, they lose all precedence and, unless out of mercy of the Apostolic See, all hope of promotion.[10]  Honorius III, reiterating Alexander's prohibition declared the penalties were incurred *latae sententiae.*[11]  It goes without saying that no such law as this exists today, nor has it for sometime, but it is worthy of note that the penalties laid down in it are similar to those prescribed for apostates today in Canon 2385 of the Code.

The next chapter punishes clerics with deposition and religious with graver penalties if they presume to accept secular offices or exercise civil jurisdiction.[12]  The prohibition still holds and is contained in Canon 139, § 2, but has no penal sanction attached to it.

The sixth chapter, an obvious source of Canon 2380, forbids, under pain of anathema, monks or clerics to engage in business for money or to have firms held either by clerics or laymen in their name.[13]

The Fifth Book contains two laws, both regarding apostates, and both responses given by Honorius III, one to the Archbishop of Tours, the other to the Archbishop of Lyons.  In the first he says that an obstinate apostate who will not resume his habit may be confined in such strict imprisonment that nothing but his miserable life remains to him, until he recedes from his obduracy.[14]

The other and last item from the Decretals declares that a monk ordained to a sacred order in apostasy, no matter whether he has returned and been reconciled with his Abbot or not, cannot exercise the

---

[9] Conc. Lat. II, c. 9, Mansi, 21, 528; Hardouin, 6b, 1209.

[10] C. 3, X, *ne clerici vel monachi secularibus negotiis se immisceant,* III, 50.

[11] C. 10, *ex eodem titulo.*

[12] C. 4, *ex eodem titulo.*

[13] C. 6, *ex eodem titulo.*

[14] C. 5, X, *de Apostatis et reiterantibus baptismi,* V, 9.

order so received without a dispensation from the Roman Pontiff.[15]
He incurs an irregularity reserved to the Pope.

Five items are found in the Sixth Book of Boniface VIII, and
three in the Clementines. The first in the former is a decree of Boniface himself against superiors who by threats of punishment, promises and oaths exacted, intimidate their subjects lest they report
abuses to canonical visitators. He nullifies all the punishments
threatened and promises or oaths given, forbids the superiors to act
in this manner, and commands the visitators to castigate them with
condign punishment should they disobey.[16] This is the sole source
given for Canon 2413 which contains the law today, and punishes
with deposition from office a superior who offends. The decree of
Boniface does not pertain to religious alone, but they are most affected by it.

The next is a conciliar decree of the ecumenical Second Council of
Lyons held under Gregory X in 1274. It suppressed all the mendicant orders which had sprung up since Fourth Lateran and had not
received Papal confirmation, while it condemned to gradual extinc-
tion by forbidding them to receive novices or acquire or alienate any
new houses or lands, even those which had been confirmed, excepting
Dominicans, Franciscans, Augustinians and Carmelites, and punishes anyone who acts contrary to it with excommunication.[17]

There follows a decree attributed to Alexander IV in the text,
but given in the footnote of this edition as Innocent IV's (16 June,
1244), addressed to the Friars Preachers and Friars Minor. Though
in itself a particular law it was later extended and is the primary
source of the penalty contained in Canon 2411 to be incurred by superiors who admit unfit candidates to reception or profession. The
original decree forbids under pain of excommunication the admission of anyone to profession or the acceptance of renunciation to
be made in the world, before the end of the year of probation. Under
the same censure it is forbidden to hinder anyone during that year
from passing to another institute or, unless it is clearly proven that

---

[15] C. 6, *ex eodem titulo.*

[16] C. 4, *de officio ordinario,* I, 16 in VI°.

[17] C. un., *de Religiosis Domibus,* II, 17 in VI°. Gregory X in Conc. Lugd., II.

he is professed, from returning to the world.  It further irritates receptions made contrary to these prescriptions, suspends offenders from receiving any to profession in the same order and subjects them to the penalties prescribed in the order against those guilty of the graver faults.  The next chapter gives the law of Boniface VIII extending the above prohibition to all mendicants, while permitting profession within the year to other religious.[18]

The fifth and last item from the Liber VI is a law of Boniface himself promulgated in a Roman Council in 1298 punishing with excommunication incurred *ipso facto* any professed religious who abandons his habit or undertakes studies without the permission of his superior, and includes under the same ban, all doctors who knowingly teach these religious or retain them in their schools for the study of laws and physics.[19]

The legislation on our matter contained in the Clementines is taken entirely from enactments of the Council of Vienne (1312) under Clement V himself.  The first of these laws forbids, under penalty of suspension from offices and benefices and inability to obtain the same, clerics and religious to wear, without reasonable cause, the habit and decorations, especially precious ornaments, which are the prerogative of a grade or order to which they do not belong, and it commands these precious ornaments to be sold and the price given to the poor by clerics and religious having administration of goods, or, by other religious, to the superior for conversion to pious causes.[20]

The second law pronounces excommunication *ipso facto* against religious and nuns who marry, from which censure they cannot be absolved until they separate.  This law expressly states that it in no way derogates from other penalties imposed by already existing laws against these culprits.[21]

The two following laws deal with the relations between regulars and the secular parochial clergy.  The one is in regard to tithes and excommunicates *ipso facto* religious who in sermons or otherwise

[18] C. 2, 3, *de regularibus et transeuntibus ad religionem*, III, 14, in VI°.

[19] C. 2, *ne clerici vel monachi saecularibus negotiis se immisceant*, III, 24 in VI°.

[20] C. 2, *de vita et honestate clericorum*, III, 1, in Clem.

[21] C. un., *de consanguinitate et affinitate*, IV, in Clem.

dissuade the people from giving tithes to their proper church and pastor, and commands them in their principal sermons and in hearing confessions to warn the people of their duty in conscience to render these tithes. Those who knowingly omit to do so are to be severely punished by their superiors who are hereby commanded in virtue of obedience to formulate severe penal statutes on the matter. Furthermore, if anyone knowingly neglects to form the consciences of his penitents in this matter he is to be suspended from preaching until he does so, and if he presumes to preach meanwhile he is *ipso facto* excommunicated.[22]

The final law forbids religious under pain of excommunication *latae sententiae* reserved to the Roman Pontiff to administer Extreme Unction or Viaticum to clerics or laics, or to solemnize marriage without the express permission of the pastor of the parish,[23] and prescribes two months' penance for grave fault for all who absolve reserved cases.

Even this period has not greatly enriched our particular field. Though illustrious by reason of the great canonists who filled the Papal Throne, particularly Boniface VIII; and despite the fact that three General Councils were held during it (Lyons I under Innocent IV, 1245; Lyons II under Gregory X, 1274, and Vienne under Clement V, 1311) the last of which was called particularly to deal with criminal charges against a religious order, the Knights Templars, which was suppressed during it, and that it had to condemn the errors of the Beguards and Beguines, it made relatively little contribution to the Penal Laws for Religious.

[22] C. 3, *de haereticis*, V, 3, in Clem.

[23] C. 1, *de privilegiis et excessibus privilegiatorum*, V, 7, in Clem.

## CHAPTER III

### THIRD PERIOD

### COUNCIL OF TRENT

THE period between the Clementines and the Council of Trent
was a barren period in Canon Law, despite the Councils which were
held during this time, and the several jurists who occupied the Papal
Throne. It includes the Avignon Captivity, the Western Schism
with its two and then three Papal claimants, the Council of Basle
with its schism, the corruption of the Renaissance and the deluge of
the Reformation. During the period the Councils of Constance,
Florence (Basle-Ferrara-Florence) and Fifth Lateran were held, but
from none of them do we find a contribution to our field. There
were not a few disturbances concerning religious at the time, as
John XXII's battle with the Fraticelli at the very beginning of the
period, but the condemnation of these latter was not directed at religious but at heretics. Innocent VIII, it is true, in his constitution,
"Officii Nostri" of 1491, forbidding under severe censures acts contrary to the liberty of the Church, specifically mentions regulars but
attaches no particular sanction against them.[1]

Then came the relaxation, spreading corruption, the outbreak of
Luther's rebellion, and the deluge had come. The monasteries and
religious establishments were among the first spoils of the reformers,
and many glaring defects became apparent in the light of the general
conflagration—started, be it noted, by an apostate friar, enraged because he lost a tilt to a friar of another order, and consummating his
apostasy by taking as his so-called wife a renegade nun who presented him with a numerous progeny.

When, nearly thirty years after the floodgates had first broken
open, the Council of Trent met in 1545 to launch the counter attack,
it could not of course ignore the weaknesses in the religious estab-
lishment, lately brought to light. Consequently, in its twenty-fifth

---

[1] Innocent VIII Const., *"Officii Nostri,"* 25 January, 1491, Bull. Rom. ed.
Taur-Aug., Tom. 5, XX, pp. 346-348—*Fontes,* n. 60, Vol. 1, pp. 90, 91.

and last session, it took up the question of regulars, December 3 and 4, 1563. Still, only three penal laws are found in this *ex professo* tract on regulars, and none in any other decree of the Council; and these three are surprisingly mild.

But meanwhile, after the Council had been convoked, but before it took up the question of religious discipline, Pope Paul IV had issued a constitution which contained some penal legislation against apostates from religion which could not be called mild. First, they are to be stripped of every benefice with all fruits and returns therefrom, all ranks and degrees in any faculty, and made perpetually incapable of receiving any other, and of exercising any ecclesiastical order, and perpetually suspended from and deprived of and incapable of all ecclesiastical ministry. If they make use of the benefices or their fruits or returns, they are bound to restitution and if they exercise their orders or ministry they are to be punished by condign penalties. Furthermore, superiors of the order and local ordinaries are to require the apostates to return to their monasteries and, if they refuse, coerce them after previous warning by ecclesiastical censures, corporal punishments and, if necessary, recourse to the secular arm. And if they persist in their disobedience they by that fact incur the major excommunication and are to be published as such.[2] Two years later Pius IV suspended these penalties, liberated the apostates from all censures and punishments, but commanded them to present themselves with indults, dispensations or licenses before appointed judges within six months from date of publication, failure to do which will bring back on them all the censures from which they were by that constitution liberated.[3]

When the Council of Trent did act its first penalty was inflicted on those who offended against the common life and religious poverty. It forbids private possession of all and any goods by regulars either in their own name or in the name of the convent, likewise, the concession by superiors of any immovable goods to any regular, even

---

[2] Paul IV, Const., *"Post quam,"* 20 July, 1558, Bull. Rom. ed. Taur-Aug., Tom. 6, XXIII, pp. 539, 541; apud *Fontes,* n. 93.

[3] Pius IV, Const., *"Sedis Apostolicae,"* 3 April, 1560, Bull. Rom. ed. Taur-Aug., Tom. 7, VI, pp. 16-18; apud *Fontes,* n. 96, §§ 3 and 10, Vol. I, pp. 168, 169 and 171.

for his mere use, usufruct or administration. It ordains that the administration of the monasteries' goods be under officials removable at the will of the superiors, that the use of mobile goods be granted by the superior in a manner becoming the state of poverty which they have professed, that nothing superfluous be given and nothing necessary denied, and that whoever violates these prescriptions loses for two years active and passive voice, and shall likewise be punished according to the rules and constitutions of his order.[4]

The next penalty is inflicted on fugitives, those who leave their convents without written permission of superior, and it is that these be punished by the local ordinaries as deserters of their institute. Those who undertake preaching, lecturing or any other pious work under the authority of any prelate, prince, university or community, or use any privilege or faculty conceded by such, without the permission of their own superior, are to be punished as disobedient.[5]

In the following chapter the Council reiterated the law on cloister of Boniface VIII's constitution *"Periculoso,"* declaring excommunicated those who violated it.[6] This includes evidently both externs who enter and nuns who leave it illicitly.

In the seventeenth chapter of this Session the Council touches on the question of religious profession of a nun, and decrees that the superioress of the monastery must notify the bishop a month before the profession is to take place so that he may examine the dispositions of the aspirant, and if she neglects to do this she is to be suspended from office for as long as the bishop sees fit.[7]

Finally, dealing with the question of those who have accused the validity of their own profession the Council decrees that if anyone has first put off his habit, he is not to be admitted to allege any cause whatever, but forced to return to his monastery and there punished as an apostate, meanwhile enjoying no privilege of his religion.[8]

---

[4] Conc. Trid., Sess. XXV, *de regularibus*, Cap. 2.

[5] Conc. Trid., Sess. XXV, *de regularibus*, Cap. 4.

[6] Conc. Trid., Sess. XXV, *de regularibus*, Cap. 5. For law on cloister, etc., Schaaf, V. T., *The Cloister*, Cincinnati, 1921, pp. 34-36.

[7] Conc. Trid., Sess. XXV, *de regularibus*, Cap. 17.

[8] Conc. Trid., Sess. XXV, *de regularibus*, Cap. 19.

This completes the penal law of the Council of Trent for religious. It is the law of the Decretals and this third period shows very little development since Gregory IX and Boniface VIII.  It seems that the constitutions of the particular orders were still deemed quite capable, as a whole, of taking care of the punishment of offenders within their own ranks.

## CHAPTER IV

## FOURTH PERIOD

## AFTER THE COUNCIL OF TRENT

THIS fourth and last period, from the Council of Trent to the promulgation of the Code (1563-1918) is the second longest and far the richest of any of our periods. It seems best to take these sources as nearly as possible in chronological order, and without regard to whether they are papal or congregational, general decrees or particular responses, noting however, what their nature is.

The earliest of these is the Constitution, *"Circa Pastoralis,"* of Pope St. Pius V of May 29, 1566,[1] in which he obliges nuns to observe the papal cloister of Boniface VIII, and orders that they be compelled to do so by ecclesiastical penalties. His Constitution, *"Decori,"* of February 1, 1570, definitely decrees excommunication against violators of the cloister either by entering or leaving.[2] He dealt with the cloister of men in the Constitution, *"Regularium,"* of October 24, 1566, punishing superiors who admitted or introduced women into the cloister with deprivation of office and of passive voice, and with suspension *a divinis.*[3] His successor, Gregory XIII, added to this penalty that of excommunication in his constitution, *"Ubi Gratiae."* [4]

The next law is a decree of the Sacred Congregation of the Council of March 15, 1596, urged by Clement VIII, concerning the ordinations of regulars. It commanded that when regular superiors licitly sent their subjects to bishops other than the diocesan bishop,

---

[1] S. Pius V, Const., *"Circa Pastoralis,"* 29 May, 1556—*Fontes,* n. 112.

[2] S. Pius V, Const., *"Decori,"* 1 February, 1570—Bull. Rom., 7, 450; 29 January, 1570; Bull. Rom., 7, 808; *Fontes,* n. 133.

[3] S. Pius V, Const., *"Regularium,"* 24 October, 1566; Bull. Rom. 7, 487—*Fontes,* n. 115.

[4] Gregory XIII, Const., *Ubi Gratiae,* 13 June, 1575; Bull. Rom. 8, 113.

they must express in the dismissorial letters the reason for doing so, and if they neglect this they incur the penalty of privation of office, dignity, administration, active and passive voice, and any other penalty the Pope decides upon, all reserved to him.[5]  This law was cited as urging, and applied in responses of the same Congregation in 1708 [6] and again in 1733.[7]

In 1598 a decision of the Sacred Congregation of Bishops and Regulars gave the local ordinaries authority to compel by penalties and censures regulars having the care of souls to attend the diocesan conferences or *collationes*,[8] which the same Congregation had a few years earlier ordered held in each diocese.  These conferences begun by St. Charles Borromeo around 1560 were made of obligation by the Decree of this Congregation of July 1, 1579 (Lucana).[9]

The following year in a decree, *"Nullus Omnino,"* of July 25, 1599, Pope Clement VIII repeats the law of the Council of Trent regarding the common life, declares the penalties of the Council and "others much graver according to the judgment of superiors" will be incurred *ipso facto* by those who violate it.  It states in particular that all, even superiors, are bound to the common table and identical fare, and allowed nothing else, save because of infirmity; and those who sin in this matter must fast for that day on bread and water.[10]

The same Pontiff in his rather long and detailed Constitution, *"Cum ad Regularem,"* concerning the admission and training of novices and their admission to profession, prescribes privation of all offices which they have obtained and graver penalties, as the pun-

[5] *Fontes*, n. 2294.

[6] S. C. EE & RR Caputquen, 28 January, and 11 February, 1708, ad 2am *Fontes*, n. 3060.

[7] S. C. EE & RR Brixiensis, 28 November and 13 December, 1733, ad 3am and 5am—*Fontes*, n. 3411.

[8] S. C. EE & RR Patavina, 27 May, 1598—*Fontes*, n. 1572.

[9] Vermeersch-Creusen (Vol. I, Pars 2, 5th ed., p. 219), attributes their institution to St. Charles.

[10] Clement VIII, decr., *"Nullus Omnio,"* 25 July, 1599, Bull. Rom. ed Taur-Aug., Tom. 10, CCLIII, p. 663, 664.

ishment for superiors who act against the prescriptions of this Constitution.[11]

The next year the Sacred Congregation of Bishops and Regulars issued a declaration in a particular case to the effect that the Mercederian Order was to be compelled to take back an apostate who sought to return, but that he was to be subjected to the constitutional and canonical punishments.[12]  This can scarcely be called a penal law, but is indicative of the mind of the Church at that time in regard to straying religious.  They are to be sought after, pursued, compelled to return if possible, even by aid of the secular power, and once returned, subjected to the penalties incurred through their offense.  This institute, however, cannot refuse to accept these returning prodigals, and it is furthermore not to dismiss its subjects if this can possibly be avoided.  That this was the spirit at the time is borne out by two later decrees, one of this same Congregation,[13] and the other of the Congregation of the Council.[14]  That this spirit prevails even today, at least in the theory of law, is apparent from the fact that the Code rejected the proposal of the Schema to include among offenses carrying *ipso facto* dismissal, apostasy from religion.[15]

On February 27, 1610, the Sacred Congregation of the Council declared that superioresses who neglected to notify the bishop of the approaching profession of novices incurred the suspension from office decreed by the Council of Trent only if the profession actually took place.  If it did not take place the bishop was not to molest her.[16]

The next addition to the store of Penal Law for Religious was the Apostolic Letter, *"Ex Debito,"* of Urban VIII.  Interdicting in the strongest terms all trading or any other kind of business transactions

---

[11] Clement VIII, Const., *"Cum ad Regularem,"* 19 March, 1603—*Fontes*, n. 189.

[12] S. C. EE & RR, *"Ordinis B. M. V. de Mercede,"* 10 February, 1604—*Fontes*, n. 1630.

[13] S. C. EE & RR, *Episcopo Vilnensis*, June, 1726, Bizzarri, p. 320.

[14] S. C. Conc., 21 September, 1624, § 4—*Fontes*, n. 2554.

[15] *Cf.* Canon 646, § 1, and Decree of S. C. de Rel., 16 Maii, 1911, n. 18, *Acta Apostolicae Sedis*, III, 1911, 235-238.

[16] S. C. Conc., *Brundusina*, 27 February, 1610—*Fontes*, n. 2385.

to every religious of every kind he attaches to his prohibition the penalties of excommunication *latae sententiae,* privation of active and passive voice and every office, degree or dignity of whatever kind, and inability to obtain them, and, furthermore, the loss of the merchandise and money obtained therefrom. And moreover the superiors are commanded under the same penalties to take action against those who are guilty.[17] This prohibition was occasioned by certain abuses on the Indian Missions which it is not within our scope to review. The same Bull carries an excommunication in paragraph 5 against anyone who hinders missionaries from going to the Far East, but though it refers to religious, the penalty is against anyone, hence not proper to religious.

Some years later the question of the diocesan conferences or *Collationes* already noted again came to the fore. A certain bishop conceived the idea of revoking faculties to hear confessions from all those, especially the regulars, who would not attend, and sought advice of the Sacred Congregation in the matter. In its response under date of September 3, 1650, the Congregation "thought that the bishop could only force secular pastors and regulars exercising the care of souls to attend . . . ; others he could exhort by admonitions but not by force." [18]

Shortly afterwards the Constitution, *"In Supremo,"* of Innocent X appeared. It was a severe denunciation of the *"Crimen falsi"* or forgery (of papal documents, or those of the Apostolic See) and renewed all the old penalties while adding new ones—confiscation of all goods, offices, rights; but though it specifically mentions religious "of every kind" as contracting all penalties whether general or special, for this crime, it does not add a single penalty for them alone.[19]

Clement IX, shortly after his accession, found it necessary to reiterate the prohibitions and penal sanctions of the Letter, *"Ex Debito,"* of Urban VIII against carrying on trade, especially in the Indies.

---

[17] Urban VIII, litt. ap., *"Ex Debito,"* 22 February, 1633, § 8, Bull. Rom. ed. Taur-Aug., Tom. 14, CDLVII, pp. 322, 323.

[18] S. C. Conc., *"Forosempronis,"* 3 September, 1650—*Fontes,* n. 2710.

[19] Innocent X, Const., *"In Supremo,"* 18 April, 1653, Bull. Rom. ed. Taur-Aug., Tom. 15, CLXIV, p. 711, apud *Fontes,* n. 234.

The only additional penalties were left to the judgment of the proper authorities in individual cases, but the institute to which the culprit belonged could no longer devote to its own missions the money or goods forfeited by him in punishment for his crime.[20]

The Sacred Congregation of the Council on May 11, 1669, in the decree, *"Nullius,"* reaffirmed an old law of Sixtus V forbidding regulars to have access to, or visit and converse with, nuns or others dwelling within the cloister, under penalty of excommunication, deprivation of office and of active and passive voice, which could be inflicted by the ordinary as a delegate of the Holy See.[21] This penalty, with the possible exception of the excommunication, was in force until the Code.

Under date of August, 1707, there appears in the Collectanea of the Sacred Congregation of Bishops and Regulars a curious penal law. It forbids the exercise by religious or in religious houses of "venal aromatic acts," which apparently means the manufacture of drugs, perfumes and patent medicines, excluding chemicals. The penalty was suspension *"a divinis,"* and privation of active and passive voice and offices, without any declaration.[22] It would be interesting to know what brought about such a law, but as it has disappeared and is not a source of a present law as such, its history is lost.

The same Congregation, some years afterward, gave the response cited above to the Bishop of Vilna who wished to dismiss a Visitandine nun who was disturbing the whole community by the "continual militant uneasy hardness of her head, her irreligious morals and frequent scandals." He was told to coerce her to live religiously by the remedies of law within the cloister rather than dismiss her.[23]

From Pope Benedict XIV, himself a great canonist and the most learned of all the Popes, we have three contributions. The first merely states that religious pastors, as such, are bound to the same

---

[20] Clement IX, Const., *"Sollicitudo,"* 17 June, 1669, Bull. Rom. ed., Taur-Aug., Tom. 17, CXII, pp. 799, 800, apud *Fontes,* n. 243.

[21] S. C. C. decr. *Nullius,* 11 May, 1669; Pallotini, XIV, p. 299.

[22] S. C. EE & RR, August, 1707, Bizzarri, n. 238.

[23] S. C. EE & RR, *Episcopo Vilnensis,* June, 1726—Bizzari, p. 320.

obligations toward the bishop as are secular pastors, including penalties.[24]

His second contribution goes back to the matter of ordinations of
regulars.  Apparently the decrees of Clement VIII and the Congregation of the Council had come to be neglected or too easily circum-
vented, so Benedict, having as he says, experienced this neglect as
Archbishop of Bologna, now puts a three-headed penal sanction on
the law.  The religious superiors incur privation of offices and dig-
nities, and active and passive voice; the men ordained incur irregularity if they exercise the order thus illicitly received, and the
ordaining prelate incurs that against those who ordain alien subjects
without dismissorial letters.  He declares that these are the canonical
sanctions and are incurred *ipso facto.*[25]

His third and last point relates to religious who challenge the
validity of their profession.  He declares that the penalties incurred
by those who contract a new marriage before the final sentence of
nullity of the first marriage has been pronounced are also incurred
by religious who leave their institute or take off their habit before
final sentence of nullity of their profession, and they fall, too, under
the penalties for apostasy.  Likewise those who have been granted
one resolution for restitution *in integrum* in this matter incur the
penalty for apostasy if they leave the cloister or take off their habit
before the second is granted.  A final anathema is hurled against all
who force or aid in forcing unwilling subjects to enter religion or make
profession, though this is not properly a penal law for religious as
it applies to everyone.[26]

A decree of the Sacred Congregation of Bishops and Regulars addressed to the Order of St. Augustine in the last year of Benedict
XIV's reign declares that regulars who flee to a house of another
order are to be returned to their own prelates, unless they are liable
by reason of crimes committed, to corporal punishment, life imprison-

---

[24] Benedict XIV, Const., *"Firmandis,"* 6 November, 1744, Benedict XIV,
Bull. ed. Prati, Tom. (CIX), pp. 452, 453, apud *Fontes*, n. 349.

[25] Benedict XIV, Const., *"Impositi Nobis,"* 27 February, 1747, §§ 9, 11; Benedict XIV, Bull. Prati et., Tom. 2 (XXVII), pp. 166, 167, apud *Fontes*, n. 376.

[26] Benedict XIV, Const., *"Si datam,"* 4 March, 1748, §§ 13, 20, 22; Benedict
XIV, Bull. Prati ed., Tom. 2, p. 334-337—*Fontes*, n. 385.

ment, death, or the galleys, in which case the right of sanctuary must prevail. In cases of ordinary punishments, however, they are to be returned to their own religious houses, and if either the fugitive refuses to return or the prelate to return him, they incur the penalties of apostates and those receiving apostates, which is excommunication reserved to the Supreme Pontiff.[27]

A period of ninety years elapsed between the legislation just quoted and the next following. Meanwhile the Church had passed through the cataclysm of the French Revolution and Napoleonic Wars, and the religious life, like everything else, had emerged much changed. A new Congregation, *"Super Statu Regularium,"* had appeared and though it was to be short-lived it enacted the first penal legislation for religious since the Pontificate of Benedict XIV. In a decree, *"Romani Pontifices,"* of January 25, 1848, under Pius IX this Congregation laid down certain rules for reception of postulants to the habit, and it ends its decree with a penal sanction against any religious of any rank who acts against its tenor. He incurs *ipso facto* privation of offices and of active voice and perpetual inability to obtain any, from which the Holy See alone can dispense him.[28]

And this brings us down to the Constitution, *"Apostolicae Sedis,"* of Pope Pius IX, the forerunner of the Code. The Constitution, it is true, only deals with censures *latae sententiae;* it did not reduce to one all penal laws as the Code does, for it left standing the excommunications of the Council of Trent, and most important of all for our subject, all *latae sententiae* censures for the internal rule of religious institutes in so far as they were actually in force at the time (1869). Whether this meant the general law for all religious or particular laws was never clear, and now matters not at all.[29] The Code swept away all former general penal laws and that is all that matters since 1918.

---

[27] S. C. EE & RR, *"Ordinis Sti. Augustini,"* 11 August, 1758, Bizzarri, p. 330—*Fontes,* n. 1875.

[28] S. C., Super Statu Regularium, 25 January, 1848—*Fontes,* n. 1873, 3; Bizzarri, p. 832.

[29] Smith, S. B., *Elements of Ecclesiastical Law,* Vol. III; *Ecclesiastical Punishments,* part 2, sect. 2, art. 5, p. 319ff.

In the Constitution, *"Apostolociae Sedis,"* of October 12, 1869,[80] the following penalties against religious are listed:

II. Excommunication *latae sententiae* reserved to the Roman Pontiff against:

6° Nuns leaving the cloister outside the causes and form prescribed by St. Pius V in his Constitution, *"Decori."*

7° Women violating the cloister of regular men, and superiors or others admitting them.

10° Those guilty of real simony on account of entrance into religion.

14° Religious presuming to administer to clergy or laity the Sacraments of Extreme Unction or Viaticum without the permission of the pastor.

III. Excommunication *latae sententiae* reserved to bishops or ordinaries.

1° Clerics in sacred orders, or regulars or nuns presuming to contract marriage after a solemn vow of chastity; and all presuming to contract marriage with them.

V. Suspension *latae sententiae* reserved to the sovereign Pontiff.

5° Expelled religious dwelling outside religion incur *ipso jure* perpetual suspension from the exercise of orders.

Of these six laws one, that regarding religious administering Extreme Unction and Viaticum, here changed from its original to exclude solemnizing matrimony, has vanished completely under the Code; another, the one regarding simony, is now included in the general canon on simony, while the excommunication here reserved to the bishop in the case of regulars who marry is now reserved *"simpliciter"* to the Holy See.

From the promulgation of the *Apostolicae Sedis* until after the work of codification had actually begun (1904) the only new penal legislation for religious came from interpretations of that constitution emanating from the Holy Office. There were three such. The first, December 4, 1872, declared that the censures pronounced against religious engaging in commerce by Urban VIII and Clement IX were

---

[80] *Fontes,* n. 552.

still in force after the *Apostolicae Sedis.*[81]  This incidentally would seem to confirm the view of those who held that the exception mentioned above for censures concerning religious meant those in the general law for all religious.

The second was a response to the Bishop of Ratisbon dated December 22, 1880.  The first query was whether the excommunication of clerics in major orders, regulars and nuns pronounced in the constitution against them for contracting marriage held when they only attempted civil marriage, and the response was in the affirmative. The other, the third in the list, asked whether after the constitution an immemorial custom of allowing nuns to go out of their cloister otherwise than according to the constitution, *"Decori,"* of Pius V could be maintained, and the response was in the negative.[82]

The last was a response given January 13, 1892, to the question of whether or not clerics in sacred orders, regulars or nuns incur excommunication if they attempt to marry in case they have another impediment, as for example, affinity or consanguinity besides that of solemn vows, and the answer was that they incur.[83]

After the work of codification had actually gotten under way three decrees of the Sacred Congregation of Religious contained penal legislation.

In the instruction of July 30, 1909, the Sacred Congregation forbade the consumption of the capital of any dowries of sisters or nuns under any pretext of utility, agreement or anything else, as long as the respective nuns or sisters live, under penalties determined by law. It further states that violators of the prescription contained in this instruction, are to be gravely punished, and if the violation concerns those things which either by common law or the present instruction require the apostolic *beneplacitum* they are subject *ipso facto* to the penalties inflicted on alienators of ecclesiastical goods.[84]

[81] *Acta Sanctae Sedis,* Vol. VII, pp. 317, 318, Collectanea S. C. de Prop. Fid., n. 1398.

[82] *Acta Sanctae Sedis,* Vol. XV, pp. 536, 539, Collectanea S. C. de Prop. Fid., n. 1544.

[83] *Acta Sanctae Sedis,* Vol. XXIV, pp. 625, 626, Collectanea S. C. de Prop. Fid., n. 1777.

[84] *Acta Apostolicae Sedis,* Vol. I (1909), pp. 695-699, S. C. de Rel., 30 July, 1909.

On the sixteenth of May, 1911, the Congregation published a lengthy decree, number 18, of which gives a list of delicts to which the penalty of *ipso facto* dismissal is attached:

(a)  Public apostasy from the Catholic Faith.

(b)  Apostasy from the order or institute, unless the religious returns within three months.

(c)  Flight from the monastery with one of the opposite sex.

(d)  Attempting civil or even celebrating valid marriage as in the case of simple vows.

Number 20 of the same decree prescribes that all religious thus *ipso facto* expelled remain perpetually suspended if they be in sacred orders, until absolved by competent authority.  Others cannot ascend to higher orders without permission of the Holy See; and none can return to their own or another order or congregation without special permission of the Holy See.[35]

It might be noticed that the above decree differs from Canon 646 in one point, namely, that apostasy from the institute does not incur *ipso facto* dismissal, marking a swing back to older ideas.  Furthermore, the prohibition to return is no longer in vogue, another reversion to more ancient discipline.

The last penal legislation before the Code is contained in a decree of the Sacred Congregation dated February 3, 1913.  It regards the liberty of conscience of religious women and ordains that if any religious desires the extraordinary confessor it is not lawful for any superior either herself or through others, directly or indirectly to inquire the reason, refuse the petition either by words or actions, or for any reason to show herself to be displeased; and if she does so, let her be admonished by her proper ordinary; if she sins the same way again let her be deposed by him, the Sacred Congregation of Religious having first been heard, however.

All religious women are forbidden to discuss in any way the confessions of their companions, or to dare to criticize those sisters who

----

[35] *Acta Apostolicae Sedis*, Vol. III (1911), pp. 237, 238, S. C. de Rel., 16 May, 1911.

make their confessions to other than the deputed confessor. Otherwise, let them be punished by the superior or by the ordinary.[36]

At last, in 1917, came the Code sweeping away all general penal legislation not contained in the Code itself. Now for the first time it became possible to pick out clear-cut, distinct laws, succinctly put, and authentically official. The divisions into parts, titles, chapters were merely for the more orderly treatment of subjects in hand; the laws were the individual canons, not of course entirely independent, but nevertheless, a law in itself. There are now twenty of these containing penal legislation concerning religious—those set down at the outset—and these form the nearest approach to a Penal Code for Religious that has been attained.

[36] *Acta Apostolicae Sedis*, Vol. V (1913), pp. 62-64, S. C. de Rel., 3 February, 1913.

# PART II

COMMENTARY ON THE PRESENT LAW

OFFENSES AGAINST THE GENERAL LAWS OF THE
CHURCH

CHAPTER I

AGAINST THE FAITH ITSELF

### ARTICLE 1. APOSTASY

**Canon 646, § 1, n. 1. Ipso facto habendi sunt tanquam legitime dimissi religiosi:**
**1°. Publici apoststae a fide catholica.***

THIS law which is first found in a decree of the Sacred Congregation of Religious dated May 16, 1911,[1] applies to all religious without distinction whether men or women, clerical or lay, of solemn or simple vows, perpetual or temporary, of pontifical or diocesan institutes, and even to those societies living in common without vows.[2] The very fact of committing the crimes herein enumerated—in this case, that of public apostasy from the Catholic Faith—brings with it immediately the penalty of dismissal. The offense, of course, must be public; that is, not only external or public by nature, but public in fact and publicly known according to Canon 2195, § 1, n. 3. Secret apostasy, therefore, even though external and externally manifested does not suffice [3] although it is not necessary that one formally em-

---

* The following religious are *ipso facto* regarded as lawfully dismissed:

1° Religious who have publicly apostatized from the Catholic Faith.

[1] S. C. *de Rel.*, 16 May, 1911—A. A. S., III (1911), 237.

[2] Canon 681.

[3] Schäfer, Timotheus, *De Religiosis* (Münster, 1931), p. 754, n. 576; Pruemmer, D., *Manuale Juris Canonici* (Rome, 1927), q. 257; Bastien, P., *Directoire Canonique a l'usage des Congregations a voeux simples* (Bruges, 1923), p. 128, nn. 1, 2; Cocchi, G., *Commentarium in Codicem Juris Canonici* (Rome, 1929), Book 2, n. 195A; Hippolytus a S. Familia, "De Dimissione Religiosorum," in *Analecta Ordinis Carmelitarum Discalceatorum*, IV (1930), 159.

brace a non-Catholic sect.[4]   Thus far all agree.   There is a sharp difference of opinion among authors, however, as to just who commits the crime, that is, who are classified as having *apostatized from the Catholic Faith.*

One group [5] insists that the term *apostatized* be taken here strictly as defined in Canon 1325, § 2, that is, having *totally abandoned the Christian Faith.*   The other group [6] contends that the inclusion of the word *Catholic* before *Faith* indicates that it is to be taken in a wider sense than that laid down in 1325, § 2, and includes heretics.

The arguments for the first group have been succinctly set forth in the *Analecta* of the Discalced Carmelites and in the *Commentarium pro Religiosis* by the authors cited above.   In the first place, they maintain, it is a case of dealing in *"odiosis"* and since these are to be restricted,[7] and as the law is not clear, the minimum is to be held, since in penalties the more benign interpretation is to be made.[8]   Furthermore, recourse to parallel places in the Code [9] and the constant canonical tradition distinguishes *apostasy* from *heresy* and *schism*, and re-

---

[4] Pruemmer, J. C., *Man. J. C.*, q. 257; Fanfani, D., *De Jure Religiosorum* (Rome, 1925), n. 496; Leitner, M., *Handbuch des Katholischen Kirchenrechts* (Ratisbon, 1919), pp. 461, 462; Bastien, o. c., p. 128.

[5] Blat, A., *Commentarium in Textum Codicis Juris Canonici*, Vol. II, n. 726; Leduc, A., *De Religiosis* (Rome, 1930), pp. 472, 473; Cocchi, *l. c.*; Bruaert, Simenon, *Manuale Juris Canonici* (Gandae et Leodii, 1930), Vol. I, n. 691; De Meester, D. J. C., *Juris Canonici et Juris Canonico-Civilis Compendium* (Bruges, 1923), Vol. II, n. 1057; Bouche, J., in *Dictionnaire de Droit Canonique* (Paris, 1928), Fascicule III, "Apostasie," p. 639ff; Hippolytus a S. Familia, *Analecta Ordinis Carmelitarum Discalceatorum*, IV (1930), 159; Tabera, A., "De Dimissione Religiosorum," in *Commentarium pro Religiosis*, Vol. XI (1930), pp. 413-415.

[6] Schäfer, o. c., n. 576; Leitner, o. c., pp. 461, 462; Palombo, J., *De Dimissione Religiosorum* (Turin-Rome, 1931), n. 197; Chelodi, J., *Jus de Personis* (Trent, 1927), n. 289, n. 1; Conte a Coronata, M., *Institutiones Juris Canonici* (Turin, 1928), Vol. I, p. 845; Augustine, C., *A Commentary on the New Code of Canon Law* (St. Louis, 1922), Vol. III, p. 386; Wernz-Vidal, *De Religiosis* (Rome, 1923), n. 438; Eichmann, E., *Lehrbuch des Kirchenrechts auf Grund des Codes Juris Canonici* (Paderborn, 1926), p. 257, § 101.

[7] Canon 19, Reg. 15, R. J. in VI°.

[8] Canon 2219, § 1.

[9] Canon 18.

stricts the former to total abandonment of the Christian Faith. They likewise argue that nowhere is to be found any distinction between apostasy from the Christian Faith and the Catholic Faith, because as St. Thomas teaches [10] apostasy is not a determined species of infidelity, but a certain aggravating circumstance. They cite Canons 985, 1065, 1240, 1453, 1470, 2314, 2339 and 2372 as parallel places where the term apostasy is used strictly according to Canon 1325, § 2.

It must be said that the arguments are not compelling. Granting that the term *apostate* standing alone should be interpreted according to the definition of Canon 1325, § 2, it does not therefore follow that the qualifying adjective *Catholic* is to be disregarded, and this is the only place in the Code where the term *apostate from the Catholic Faith* is used. Moreover, the recourse to the literal meaning and theological significance of the term as explained by St. Thomas rather militates against their argument than for it. In the very response above quoted, St. Thomas describes the "aggravating circumstance" as a "movement of receding from the faith." [11] Thus the real distinction between an apostate and simple heretic is that the heretic may have been born and raised in heresy, knows the teaching of the Church and refuses to accept some part of it, while the apostate is one who, having formerly professed the Faith, has since abandoned it.

Now the following dilemma presents itself. Either the term Catholic must be given its proper meaning in this canon or Canon 1325, § 2, must be interpreted, contrary to the universal views of all commentators, in the theological rather than the canonical significance of the term and the parallel canons likewise, for if there is no real distinction between apostasy from the Christian and from the Catholic Faith, since the Catholic and Christian Faith are formally identical—since there is but the one formal reason of Faith—the argument of Augustine [12] and Coronata [13] seems conclusive. They argue that if one renounces even one article of faith, he becomes an

---

[10] St. Thomas Aquinas, *Summa Theologica,* IIa, IIae, q. XII, Art. I, ad 3um.

[11] St. Thomas II, IIae, q. XII, Art. 1, ad 3um.

[12] Augustine, *Commentary,* III, p. 386.

[13] Coronata, o. c., I, p. 845.

apostate, the same as if he had become a Mohammedan or free-thinker, because he has renounced the formal reason of faith (*ratio formalis fidei*) and consequently the whole faith. The fact that he has not rejected the entire material body of Christian teaching makes little difference; what he believes he no longer believes under the formal reason of faith.[14] Furthermore, in special reference to this canon, Wernz-Vidal [15] quite properly point out that it is most incongruous that one who has placed himself outside the Church by embracing an heretical sect should remain a religious, that is, in a public and juridic state in the Church. It is certainly true that there seems no more reason why a renegade to Presbyterianism, for instance, should not incur the penalty of dismissal the same as a renegade to Unitarianism—a non-Christian sect.

An argument based on this principle may be adduced from Canon 538 which requires that for valid admission to religion one be a *Catholic*. As Larraona says: It does not suffice that one be a Christian in order to be admitted as a candidate; he must necessarily be a Catholic; otherwise his admission is invalid, for no one ever doubted that a non-Catholic could not validly be admitted to religion, for the religious state is the state of perfection which necessarily supposes the Christian life in the Church. Hence non-baptized, by valid baptism in the external forum, even though catechumens, apostates from the faith, heretics or schismatics, are excluded from any admission to postulancy, novitiate or profession.[16]

The same basis required for one's admission to religion should also be required for his continuance therein and as the structure cannot be begun without the foundation of Catholicity, it seems necessary to suppose that the destruction of this foundation would bring about the destruction of the edifice.

Again, an analysis of the canons cited in support of the argument for exclusion of heretics will manifest its weakness, for, bearing in

---

[14] D'Annibale, J., "*Summula Theologiae Moralis*" (Rome, 1908), 5th ed., Vol. II, n. 7, footnote 25.

[15] Wernz-Vidal, *De Religiosis*, n. 438.

[16] Larraona, A., De Admissione in Religionem, in *Commentarium Pro Religiosis*, XV (1935), 352-357.

mind one of their arguments against the importance of the word "Catholic" namely, that the Code does not hold constantly and rigidly a precise and uniform signification of terms throughout, the argument from parallel places seems based on a weak foundation. To be specific:

1. Canon 985, treating of the subject of ordination, declares irregular *ex delicto* "apostates from the faith, heretics, schismatics." In the first place, be it noted, that this canon merely speaks of "apostates from the faith," not the Catholic Faith, but even if this distinction be passed over, apostates here may very well be taken to mean renegades to heresy.  Obviously all baptized non-Catholics are *de se* irregular *ex delicto,* for even heretics and schismatics who were in good faith are dispensed from the irregularity *ad cautelam.*[17]  The unbaptized are incapable of receiving orders.  Hence the meaning of Canon 985 may be well stated as "all baptized infidels, whether renegades from Catholicism or reared in infidelity, Christian or non-Christian" are irregular *ex delicto,* and no argument for the restricted sense is found here.

2. Canon 1065 concerns prohibiting impediments to marriage. The law having forbidden marriage of a Catholic to a baptized non-Catholic[18] in this canon ordains that "the faithful shall be deterred also from contracting marriage with those who have notoriously renounced the Catholic faith without, however, joining a non-Catholic sect, or with those who are notoriously affiliated with societies condemned by the Church."

The writer cited above[19] states quite correctly that the "renunciation of the Catholic faith in this canon and the apostasy from the Catholic faith in Canon 646, § 1, n. 1, are parallel passages.  Wrongly, however, does he conclude that the interpretation excludes renegades to heresy.  Chelodi[20] whom he cites in support of his contention seems rather to hold quite the opposite and Gas-

---

[17] Vermeersch-Creusen, *Epitome,* II, n. 257.

[18] Canon 1060.

[19] Hippolytus a S. Familia, "De Dimissione," etc., in *Anal. O. C. D.,* IV (1930), 159.

[20] Chelodi, J., *Jus Matrimoniale* (Trent, 1921), n. 66.

parri [21] Vermeersch-Creusen,[22] Ayrinhac [23] and indirectly Cerato [24] plainly include those who have ceased to be Catholics without entirely abandoning all the tenets of Christianity. And moreover the very nature of the prohibition and the reasons taken from divine law on which it is based, demand that it include all renegades from Catholicism and not merely those who have given up every vestige of Christianity. The argument, therefore, from this canon is rather against than in favor of the exclusionists.

3. Canon 1240, § 1, n. 1, denies Christian burial to "notorious apostates from the Christian faith, . . . or those notoriously enrolled in an heretical or schismatical sect." It is true that Blat [25] seems to restrict the apostasy here to total (material) rejection of the Christian Faith and Leduc [26] may be interpreted similarly, but Vermeersch-Creusen [27] quite properly places a well-defined distinction which implicitly interprets apostasy according to the theory of Augustine cited above [28] when he says that "the sin of heresy does not exclude from Christian burial unless it constitutes notorious apostasy or is accompanied by notorious enrollment in an heretical sect." [29] Thus the argument from Canon 1240 seems at least begging the question.

4. In regard to Canon 1453 which prohibits the transmission of the *jus patronatus* over benefices to "infidels, public apostates, heretics, schismatics . . . " the same exception can be taken. Although the term used is mere "public apostates" it seems begging the question to take that to mean exclusively those who have totally abandoned all the truths of Christianity, since from the nature and even

---

[21] Gasparri, Pietro Card., *Tractatus Canonicus de Matrimonio* (Typis Polyglottis Vaticanis, 1932), Vol. I, n. 479.

[22] Vermeersch-Creusen, *Epitome*, II, n. 335.

[23] Ayrinhac, H. A., *Marriage Legislation in the New Code of Canon Law.* Revised and enlarged by Rev. P. J. Lydon, D.D. (London, 1932), p. 119.

[24] Cerato, P., *Matrimonium a Codice Juris Canonici Integre Desumptum* (Patavia, 1919), n. 59, 1.

[25] Blat, *Comment.*, Vol. III, "*De Sacramentis*," n. 101.

[26] Leduc, A., *De Locis et Temporibus Sacris* (Rome, 1931), p. 193.

[27] Vermeersch-Creusen, *Epitome*, n. 549.

[28] *Cf.* Augustine, *Commentary*, III, p. 386.

[29] Vermeersch-Creusen, *Epitome*, n. 549.

wording of the law all infidels, no matter how they became such, are barred from the *jus patronatus*.

5. Canon 1470 does denote a difference between a "fall into heresy" and into "apostasy," and seems to take the latter to mean a material as well as formal abandonment of Christianity. Yet the force is taken from this argument by recourse to the one employed above by the exclusionists that "the Code does not hold constantly and rigidly a precise and uniform signification of terms." [30]

6. The same thing must be said of Canon 2314. It does seem to imply something more than a modal distinction between the heretics and apostates on whom it inflicts the penalties of paragraph one, and for whose absolution it provides in paragraph two. Nevertheless, when it is reflected that even converts who were born and raised in heresy must be absolved from the censures herein inflicted the argument loses most of its force.

7. What was said above in regard to Canons 985 and 1240 and 1453 applies also to Canon 2339 where forced Christian burial to all sorts of "infidels, apostates from the faith, heretics and schismatics . . . " is punished with excommunication. There is no reason in text or context, or from the nature of the thing, to restrict apostasy here to a complete abandonment of all Christian truth.

8. Canon 2372 pronounces suspension against anyone who "presumes to receive orders from ". . . a notorious apostate, heretic, or schismatic." The indication is quite strong that apostate here does not mean one who has completely abandoned the Christian Religion for it does not seem reasonable that one who has completely abandoned Christianity would be practising it to the extent of validly conferring orders. Moreover, it is plain what classes of bishops are meant: Catholic bishops who have renounced their faith, whether they have abandoned all the doctrines of Christianity or merely gone over to non-Catholic sects; validly consecrated bishops of heretical sects in which they were born and raised, as in the Monophysite sects of the East; validly consecrated bishops of schismatic bodies to which they have always belonged, such as, at least before the Vatican Council, the Eastern Orthodox Churches.

---

[30] Wernz-Vidal, *De Religiosis* n. 348.

Therefore, the whole argument settles itself back to whether or not apostate from the Catholic Faith in Canon 646, § 1, means the same thing as apostate who has totally abandoned the Christian faith in Canon 1325, § 2. If the words be taken as they stand in a canonical sense they do not, and under the former heretics are included. If recourse be had to the theological sense and Christian faith and Catholic Faith taken as one, then they do mean the same thing, but heretics and all others who have abandoned the *ratio formalis fidei* must be included under the term apostate in Canon 1325, § 2, an opinion not held, at least explicitly, in any work which comes to hand, but which would certainly include heretics under Canon 646, § 1.

Having considered the arguments presented, the conclusion would seem to be that, despite the assertion of the Carmelite writer [31] the opinion which includes renegades to heresy under the term "apostates from the Catholic faith" is in itself more probable, though it is not safe to include schismatics as do Coronata [32] and Eichmann [33] against Leitner [34] and Schäfer [35] for the very good reason that schism does not necessarily imply an abandonment of the *ratio formalis fidei*.

When it comes to the application and enforcement of this penalty in the external forum, it becomes another matter. The very fact that so many uphold the opposite opinion throws it into the class of doubtful laws and here their arguments concerning the restriction of things odious,[36] the more benign interpretation of penal laws [37] and the fact that there is *dubium juris* under which the law does not bind [38] make it quite impossible to enforce the penalty.[39] In prac-

---

[31] Hippolytus, a. S., Familia, *Analecta O. C. D.*, IV (1930), 159.

[32] Coronata, *Institutiones*, I, p. 845.

[33] Eichmann, *Lehrbuch des Kirchenrechts*, p. 257.

[34] Leitner, *Handbuch*, pp. 461, 462.

[35] Schäfer, *De Religiosis*, n. 576.

[36] Reg. 15, R. J., in VI°.

[37] Canon 2219.

[38] Canon 15.

[39] *Cf.* Ayrinhac, *Penal Legislation in the New Code of Canon Law* (New

tice, however, a religious who publicly fell into heresy could be summarily dismissed in accordance with Canons 653 and 668. None the less, until the point has been officially decided, such a one might claim reinstatement under Canon 672, which would be impossible were he recognized as dismissed *ipso facto* under Canon 646, § 1.[40]

### ARTICLE 2. CANON 646

THE offenses punished with *ipso jure* dismissal in virtue of Canon 646, one of which has just been dealt with, will be treated below in their proper places.[41] However, it is fitting to take up here the recent response of the Pontifical Commission for authentically interpreting the canons of the Code [42] which decided two controversies concerning this canon which have been carried on for some time. The first item of the response declared that the declaration of fact prescribed in the second paragraph of this canon was not necessary for the effectiveness of the dismissal; in other words, the dismissal takes effect as soon as the crime is committed and the declaration is merely to make it enforceable in the external forum [43] and its observance of obligation in the internal forum in all circumstances.[44] The nature of the crimes is such that they could not easily be kept secret, though secret elopement and speedy return or even secret marriage is by no means inconceivable. The dismissal would take effect at the moment the crime was consummated, but it could not be enforced externally nor would the culprit be obliged to observe it if such observance brought infamy on himself until after the declaration of fact.

York, 1920), 58; Chelodi, *Jus Poenale* (Trent, 1933), n. 23; Sole, *De Delictis et Poenis* (Rome, 1920), n. 76.

[40] Pont. Com., 30 June, 1934—A. A. S., XXVI (1934), p. 494.

[41] Flight with person of the opposite sex, Part II, Chapter VIII, Art. 3. Marriage or attempted marriage or civil bond, Part II, Chapter X, Art. 3.

[42] Pont. Com., 30 July, 1934—A. A. S., XVI (1934), 494.

[43] Canon 2232, § 1.

[44] Canon 2232. Maroto, "Annotationes 'super responso,' Pont. Com., 30 July, 1934; III, De Ret. Dismissi," *In Commentarium pro Religiosis*, XV (1934), 352-356.

The reason for doubting as to whether or not the declaration was necessary for the infliction of the penalty was because the canon used the word "suffices" in regard to it. Some interpreted this to mean that the mere commission of the offense without the declaration did not suffice; in other words, that the declaration was not merely sufficient but necessary and sufficient. That this was foreign to the sense of the canon seemed clear and is now indisputable. It merely meant that the process and decree of dismissal were not necessary in the case of these offenses, but a mere declaration of fact sufficient. As Maroto [45] remarks, the response does not free the superiors from the obligation of making the declaration, but the penalty is incurred beforehand.

The second question decided was not so apparent, and the decision ran contrary to the more common opinion of the authors. It concerned the application of Canon 672, by which dismissed religious still bound by vows are required to return to their institute and the institute is bound to receive them back after three years of amendment. The Commission decided that this prescription did not apply to those *ipso facto* dismissed for the crimes mentioned in Canon 646, § 1.[46]

Some years ago Larraona [47] proposed the opinion that Canon 672 applied only to the minor delicts treated in Canon 671 and not to the graver crimes summarily dealt with in Canon 670 by deprivation of the ecclesiastical habit, amongst which crimes are those carrying *ipso facto* dismissal in virtue of Canon 646. The recent response of the Commission leaves untouched the question regarding the other graver crimes and simply states that Canon 672 does not apply to those dismissed *ipso facto* in virtue of Canon 646. The arguments therefore of Larraona which apply to these three crimes may well be set forth here as giving the clearest reason for what seems at first sight a restrictive interpretation on the part of the Commission.

His first argument is that from the text of the canon it applies

---

[45] Maroto, *l. c.*

[46] Pont. Com., 30 July, 1934—A. A. S., XXVI (1934), 494.

[47] "Quaestio Canonica," *Commentarium pro Religiosis,* III (1922), 318-329.

only to those mentioned in Canon 671, namely, those guilty of lighter offenses than the ones punished in Canons 646 and 670, and that it considers the gradual amendment of the former while ignoring the possibility of amendment on the part of these latter, and he feels the reference to a benevolent bishop in the second paragraph confirms this argument, inasmuch as those dismissed for the major crimes have no need for nor are worthy of a benevolent bishop.

The next argument, taken from the nature of the case juridically considered, shows that the effect of dismissal for some minor cause should differ in degree from the effect of dismissal on account of an offense which is so totally opposed to the essentials of religious life as the crimes punished by Canon 646. As he says, it is not reasonable to suppose that the qualified dismissal for the latter is no more severe than the simple dismissal for the former, or that they can and should both be received back the same way.

Moreover, in regard to clerics, the fact that the dismissal carries with it in virtue of Canon 670 perpetual prohibition to wear the ecclesiastical habit, which is a perpetual vindictive penalty reserved to the Roman Pontiff [48] and can be dispensed only by a favor which the law cannot presume, and which in its turn brings with it irregularity, inability to exercise legitimate ecclesiastical acts, and privation of clerical privileges—the fact, as said, that all these penalties flow from the dismissal makes it most improbable that an institute would be obliged to receive back one bound by so many penalties. And as the law cannot suppose that they will be dispensed within three years, it can scarcely impose the obligation of receiving the guilty ones back.

Finally, since the law makes no provision for the gradual amendment of such parties, nor for their care and observation as it does for those guilty of minor offenses, and since moreover it does not even prescribe a charitable subsidy for them, it seems to liberate

---

[48] The statement which follows, *viz.*, that this penalty carries with it irregularity and inability to exercise legitimate ecclesiastical acts cannot be sustained. It is not mentioned in Canons 984 and 985 where irregularities are enumerated taxatively. Apostasy and marriage or attempted marriage by religious does render the culprit irregular, but flight with a woman does not. It does, however, carry with it suspension in virtue of Canon 2386.

the institute from all care for or connection with those who have committed crimes so contrary to the essence of the religious state, and consequently freed it from all obligation of taking them back.

As Maroto [49] rightly remarks, the decision of the Commission also liberates the dismissed from the obligation of returning, not as a favor to them but as a favor to the institute, since it is obviously impossible for them to return if the institute is not to receive them.

[49] Maroto, *l. c.*

# CHAPTER II

## OFFENSES AGAINST ECCLESIASTICAL AUTHORITY

THIS chapter treats of four canons which prescribe special penalties for religious offending against ecclesiastical authority in three ways.  First are those who offend against the authority of the superiors (Canon 2331, § 2), next those who offend against the Church's authority by using civil power to restrict it or hinder its exercise (Canon 2334), and finally, those who enroll in organizations, such as the Masons, directly working against that authority (2335).  The penalties against religious of the last two classes are found in Canon 2336.

### ARTICLE 1.  AGAINST THE AUTHORITY OF SUPERIORS
### Canon 2331, § 2

**Canon 2331, § 2. Conspirantes vero contra auctoritatem Romani Pontificis eiusve Legati vel proprii Ordinarii aut contra eorum legitima mandata, itemque subditos ad inobedientiam erga ipsos provocantes, censuris aliisve poenis coerceantur; et . . . voce activa et passiva atque officio, si [sint] religiosi, priventur.***

Although this penalty against religious is not found in the immediate pre-Code law, Canon 18, of the Council of Chalcedon (A. D. 451)[1] prescribes a very similar penalty against "monks conspiring against bishops and clergy," as stated above in the first chapter.[2]

---

*Canon 2391, § 2.  Those conspiring against the authority of the Roman Pontiff or of his Legate or of their own Ordinary or against their legitimate mandates, and also those inciting subjects to disobedience towards them, are to be coerced by censures or other penalties; and . . . if they are religious, deprived of active and passive voice and of office.

[1] Council of Chalcedon, Canon 18—Mansi, 7, 378; apud Gratianum, c. 23, C. CXI, q. 1.

[2] Supra Part 1, Chap. 1, note 11.

The first paragraph of the canon in hand treats of simple disobedience towards the Roman Pontiff, ordinary and others, and contains no special penalty against religious guilty of such offenses. The second paragraph treating of the graver crime of conspiracy and inciting others to rebellion adds the special sanction for religious, namely, loss of office, and of the right to vote or to be voted for. Naturally, the crime of conspiracy and of inciting others to disobedience is punished by heavier penalties than mere obstinate disobedience as it manifests a deeper malice, is more subversive of common order, and has more extensive effects.[8]

Conspiracy is had when two or more form common plans to act, in this case, against the authority mentioned, that is of the Pope, his legate,[4] whether he be legate *a latere*,[5] nuncio or internuncio or apostolic delegate,[6] or their proper ordinary [7] or against the legitimate orders, in its widest sense, of these authorities.

It should be noted, however, that the mandates or orders, of whatever character they may be, must be legitimate, that is, they must come from one who has the authority to give them, concern matter over which he has authority, and be in conformity with the laws of God and the Church and the constitutions of the institute, if the case be of a religious ordinary. As regards the Roman Pontiff, there can be no question  Any order of his is legitimate unless it contravenes divine law. The orders of his legates must be within the field of their jurisdiction. In like manner, mandates which exceed the ordinary's power are not legitimate, and hence not contemplated by this canon.

Hence those who thus conspire among themselves to obstruct

---

[8] Ayrinhac, *Penal Legislation*, n. 245; Sole, o. c., n. 355; Chelodi, *Jus Poenale*, n. 69, 3.

[4] Canon 265.

[5] Canon 266.

[6] Canon 267.

[7] The proper ordinary for exempt clerical religious is the major superior, *i. e.*, general, provincial, or abbot, excluding the abbot primate and abbot president of monastic congregations. Canons 198, 488, n. 8; and 501, § 3. For nonexempt religious the proper ordinary is the local ordinary of the territory in which their house of assignment is located.

the legitimate exercise of the authority above referred to, no matter by what means, and those, even single individuals, who attempt by words, acts, writing or any other means to spread disobedience to such authority, incur the penalties of the canon. As it is evident from the wording of the canon, it makes no difference whether or not they actually spread disobedience. The attempt constitutes the crime in this case.[8]

One does not become liable to the penalty in virtue of this canon if the conspiracy or agitation is against other authority, as for instance, that of local superiors, or even major superiors who are not ordinaries, namely, those of non-exempt institutes, nor if it is against the authority or mandates of another ordinary. Thus an exempt religious who conspired against or incited subjects of the local ordinary to disobedience against him would not fall under the law of this canon, as the use of the intensive reflexive *ipsos*, "these very ones," referring to their own ordinaries (*proprii ordinarii*) clearly shows.

The penalty is privation of active and passive voice, that is, the right to vote or to be elected to office, and even privation of office if the culprit holds office. This is a vindicative penalty reserved to the Holy See.[9] It is *ferendae sententiae* but, from the use of the jussive subjunctive the infliction is preceptive. That is, the penalty is not incurred by the very fact of committing the crime, but it must be inflicted by a judge or superior. However, it is left to the prudence and conscience of the one who inflicts it to moderate it according to circumstances which may have diminished the imputability of the act, or even to abstain from inflicting it altogether if sufficient punishment has been inflicted or full amendment already procured.[10] This may be said of all the punishments for religious treated in this chapter.

---

[8] Chelodi, *Jus Poenale*, n. 69, 3; Ayrinhac, *Penal Legislation*, n. 245.

[9] Canons 2291, n. 11°, and 2237, § 1, n. 3.

[10] Canon 2223, § 3.

### ARTICLE 2. OFFENSES AGAINST THE RIGHTS OF THE CHURCH

### Canon 2336

**Canon 2336, § 1. . . . . religiosi autem [qui delictum commiserunt de quo in Canons 2334, 2335, praeter poenis citatis canonibus statutas], privatione officii et vocis activae ac passivae aliisque poenis ad normam constitutionum plectantur.***

**Canon 2334, § 1. Excommunicatione latae sententiae speciali modo Sedi Apostolicae reservata plecuntur:**

**1° Qui leges, mandata, vel decreta contra libertatem aut iura Ecclesiae edunt.**

**2° Qui impediunt directe vel indirecte exercitium iurisdictionis ecclesiasticae sive interni sive externi fori, ad hoc recurrentes ad quamlibet laicalem potestatem.****

There is a general agreement amongst authors as to the interpretation of this canon, with one or two disputes on minor points. All agree that the phrase "laws, mandates or decrees" includes everything of a legislative or regulatory nature whether it be of the supreme authority of the nation, minor provincial or municipal authority or even local police ordinances. Some [18] include the sentences

---

* Canon 2336, § 1. Religious [who commit the crimes mentioned in Canons 2334, 2335, besides the penalties prescribed in those canons] are to be punished by privation of office and of active and passive voice, and other penalties according to the norm of the constitutions.

** Canon 2334. They are punished by excommunication *latae sententiae* reserved in a special way to the Apostolic See:

1° Who enact laws, mandates or decrees agains the liberty or rights of the Church.

2° Who directly or indirectly impede the exercise of ecclesiastical jurisdiction either in the internal or external forum, by having recourse to any lay power for this purpose.

[18] Sole, o. c., n. 359; Cappello, F., *De Censuris*, n. 255, 242, 262; Blat, *Commentarium*, Vol. V, n. 175.

of judges even in particular cases, while others [14] expressly exclude these on the ground that since they regard particular cases, they do not partake of the nature of law. It may be answered that they need not partake of the nature of a law to come under the heading of "mandate" or "decree," and all agree that when a judge merely declares what the law is he is not amongst those referred to. If, however, the decree is not merely the statement of an already existing law, but a regulation of his own, it does seem to be included in this canon.

As regards the *edentes* or those who *enact* the laws, decrees, etc., it is quite well agreed, against Cerato [15] that they are the ones who possess the power formally to make the laws or decrees, that is, have the necessary legislative or administrative power, such as monarchs, senators, members of parliament, governors, prefects or even minor administrators. When the concurrence of more than one person, whether physical or moral, is required for the formal enactment of a law or decree, as for instance, passage by both houses of Congress and approval by the president, all concurring, in this case all the representatives, and senators who voted in favor of the law, and the president who signed it are considered as enacting the law. When it is submitted to popular referendum, all who vote in favor of it are considered as enacting it. While this is not so clear and somewhat disputed, it is certain that they incur the penalties as coöperators according to Canons 2209 and 2231. All agree that those who execute the laws or decrees, or those who merely materially publish them or spread knowledge of them are not included under the penalties of the canons, nor do those who urge and counsel them, unless their activities be such as to render them coöperators.[16]

---

[14] Ayrinhac, H., *Penal Legislation in the New Code of Canon Law* (New York, 1920), n. 253a; Cipolini, A., *De Censuris Latae Sententiae* (Turin, 1925), n. 27.

[15] Cerato, P., *Censurae Vigentes* (Patavia, 1921), 74e, who, while admitting that senators, deputies and the like incur the penalties as coöperators, insists that only those who sign the law giving it final sanction are considered as *edentes.*

[16] *Cf. Sole,* o. c., n. 359; Ayrinhac, *Penal Legislation,* n. 253a; Cappello, o. c., n. 255; Blat, *Comment.,* V, n. 175; Vermeersch-Creusen, *Epitome,* III, n. 534;

The rights and liberties of the Church here spoken of are to be taken in their widest sense, as the law makes no distinction. However, as Cardinal Lega points out, it is the rights and liberty of the Universal Church, and not of any particular church or members of the church unless these pertain to the rights of the whole Church.[17] These rights and liberties are both spiritual and temporal and include such things as the exercise of ecclesiastical power, both of orders and jurisdiction, the right to preach and administer the sacraments, the right to possess and administer property; the liberty of public worship, the immunity and privileges of the clergy, etc.

2°. The second number of this canon pronounces a like punishment, namely, excommunication for all and privation of office, and of active and passive voice for religious, against those who in any way, directly or indirectly, hinder the exercise of ecclesiastical jurisdiction in either the internal or external forum, by having recourse to any lay power.

As is evident, the first condition required is actually to impede the exercise, not of orders, but of jurisdiction,[18] whether ordinary or delegated,[19] judicial or voluntary,[20] of the external or internal forum, sacramental or extra-sacramental.[21] It makes no difference whether it is done directly, by impeding the act of jurisdiction itself or indirectly, by affecting the matter or persons concerned; whether the recourse is taken by the impeding party himself or through someone else.

*To hinder* is here, of course, to be understood in its strict sense; that is, to prevent the beginning or carrying out of the act of jurisdiction. It does not, therefore, include forcing the act of jurisdiction, nor harassing the one who placed the act, nor preventing the effects of the act. Hollweck [22] holds that forcing the retraction of

Chelodi, *Jus Poenale*, n. 70; Cipolini o. c., n. 27, *Tractatus de Censuris*, etc. (Dessain, editor) (Malines, 1906), pp. 59-61.

[17] Cardinal Lega, *"De Judiciis Ecclesiasticis"* (Rome, 1899), Lib. II, Vol. 3, n. 444; also Ayrinhac, *Penal Legislation*, n. 253b.

[18] Canon 196.

[19] Canon 197.

[20] Canon 201, §§ 2 and 3.

[21] Canon 196.

[22] Hollweck, J., *Die Kirchlichen Strafgesetze* (Mainz, 1899), § 132.

the act is included, while Chelodi [23] denies this, and Cappello [24] calls both opinions probable. If it be analyzed carefully, however, Chelodi's opinion seems better, for forcing the retraction of an act already completed is not impeding the act already placed, as he rightly says, but rather forcing a new act, and all agree, as stated above, that forcing the exercise of jurisdiction is not hindering it.

There is some dispute as to the extent of the term jurisdiction. Ecclesiastical jurisdiction is defined as the power of ruling and governing subjects which is derived by clerics as clerics from Christ directly or through His Vicar, the Roman Pontiff. It certainly includes the power to make laws, inflict penalties, execute sentences, confer benefices. It certainly does not include the power to perform those acts which pertain to the power of orders, such as to administer the sacraments (except penance, which does belong to jurisdiction as well as orders), bless, consecrate or perform sacred functions. The dispute is whether or not it includes the power to teach, preach, guard the faith, protect morals, buy, sell, possess, and enter contracts. Chelodi [25] holds that it does, while Cerato,[26] among others, holds that it does not. Cappello [27] calls the first opinion more true, as it is more conformable to the genuine concept of the double division of ecclesiastical power, namely, jurisdiction and orders, held in Canon Law today. This ignores entirely the dominative power. Sole,[28] quoting D'Annibale,[29] even states that the jurisdiction which regular prelates enjoy in the exempt orders is not included under this term in the present canon, while Cappello [30] states that it does not concern the exercise of privileges which religious superiors enjoy "unless it is to be referred to ecclesiastical jurisdiction." As a matter of fact, the jurisdiction which regular prelates hold is nothing else than true ecclesiastical jurisdiction,[31] and hence comes under this canon.

[23] Chelodi, *Jus Poenale*, n. 70, 3, note 2.
[24] Cappello, *De Censuris*, n. 257, 3.
[25] Chelodi, *Jus Poenale*, n. 70, 3, note 1.
[26] Cerato, o. c., n. 74f; Cipollini, o. c., n. 27.
[27] Cappello, o. c., n. 257, 2.
[28] Sole, o. c., n. 359.
[29] D'Annibale, *Commentarium in Constitutionem Apostolicae Sedis*, n. 57.
[30] Cappello, o. c., n. 257, 3.
[31] Canon 501, § 1.

The final thing to be noted is that the impeding of the exercise of jurisdiction must be by recourse to any lay power. Other modes of impeding, such as force, fraud, threats, unjust recourse to higher ecclesiastical powers are not considered or included; it must be by recourse to lay power. But any lay power is sufficient for incurring the penalties. It need not be a civil court; any administrative civil, military or police power which can prevent the exercise of jurisdiction comes under the law, and the actual prevention of the exercise of jurisdiction through recourse to such power is punished by the penalties of these canons.

The penalties against religious who are guilty of the crimes just explained are, beside the excommunication reserved in a special way to the Holy See, privation of any office they may hold, and of active and passive voice, as explained in the previous article, together with whatever other penalties their particular constitutions may contain.

### ARTICLE 3. ENROLLMENT IN MASONIC SECTS AND SIMILAR ASSOCIATIONS

**Canon 2335. Nomen dantes sectae massonicae aliisve eiusdem generis associationibus quae contra Ecclesiam vel legitimas civiles potestates machinantur, contrahunt ipso facto excommunicationem Sedi Apostolicae simpliciter reservatam.***

The penalty herein contained which falls within the scope of this dissertation is "privation of office and of active and passive voice." The offense punished by this penalty is the "giving of one's name to masonic sects or other associations of the same kind which machinate against the Church or legitimate civil powers." For religious, it falls under the jurisdiction of the Holy Office, as stated in Canon 2336, § 2, as follows:

---

*Canon 2335. Those giving their name to masonic sects or other associations of the same kind which machinate against the Church or legitimate civil powers, incur *ipso facto* excommunication reserved simply to the Apostolic See.

**Canon 2336, § 2. Insuper clerici et religiosi nomen dantes sectae massonicae aliisque similibus associationibus denuntiari debent Sacrae Congregationi S. Officii.****

Masonry was banned under pain of excommunication by Clement XII in his Constitution, *"In Eminenti,"* of April 28, 1738, and the Constitution, *"Apostolicae Sedis,"* of Pope Pius IX inflicted the penalty of excommunication simply reserved to the Holy See on those who join masonic sects, the *Carbonari* or others of the same kind who machinate against the Church or legitimate civil powers. However, the special penalty against religious in the general law of the Church is new in the Code.

The principal points to be determined in this canon are: the precise significance of the expression to "give one's name to the society"; what is meant by societies similar to the masonic sects; what is understood by "legitimate civil powers," and the precise meaning of the term "machinate" or plot.

As to the first point, *giving one's name* to the society, simply means knowingly and willingly joining or becoming a member of the organization, even though the membership be only nominal and no active part be taken or even no meeting attended.[32] Acceptance, even though only tacit, of honorary membership would seem to be included, since not active participation but voluntary enrollment is the offense punished. The degree of knowledge required for contracting the penalty is not agreed upon amongst authors. Sole [33] requires knowledge of the evil end of the society and the fact of its prohibition under pain of excommunication, and Cipollini [34] concurs, while Cerato [35] holds that knowledge of the evil end of the society is not required, provided one knows the sect to be masonic. In prac-

---

** Canon 2336, § 2. Moreover clerics and religious giving their name to masonic sects and other similar associations ought to be denounced to the Sacred Congregation of the Holy Office.

[32] Ayrinhac, H., *Penal Legislation in the New Code of Canon Law* (New York, 1920), n. 257; Sole, n. 361.

[33] Sole, o. c., n. 361.

[34] Cipollini, A., *De Censuris Latae Sententiae* (Turin, 1925), n. 40.

[35] Cerato, P., *Censurae Vigentes Ipso Facto* (Patavia, 1921), n. 55.

tice, the difficulty is not important, for there is scarcely a Catholic, and certainly no religious, who does not know all masonic sects to have an evil end, and to be forbidden under penalty, while for other societies or sects not condemned by name the knowledge of the end would certainly be required. Cerato [36] likewise holds that one who has joined in good faith incurs the penalties if he does not withdraw as soon as he becomes aware of the character of the society, while Ayrinhac [37] states that he would not incur until he affirmed his membership by a new act. Considering the strict interpretation to which penal laws are subject,[38] neither opinion seems altogether correct, as it is the giving of the name to, or in other words, enrollment in, the society that is punished, and as Quigley rightly says, a person already enrolled does not *give his name* to the society, either by simply remaining in it or even by affirming his membership by a new act.[39] Hence, he rightly concludes these latter do not incur the censure though they certainly sin gravely. As regards religious, they might fittingly be punished with privation of active and passive voice and of office, if not strictly in virtue of this canon, then in virtue of Canon 2222, using this as a guiding norm.

The canon mentions societies similar to the masons which plot against the Church or legitimate civil power, but it is not clear just what societies fall under this heading. All agree that it must be a real society, having its own statutes and officials, and a social bond uniting its members. It must be similar to the masonic sects, at least, in so far as it plots against the Church or State. Some authors [40] consider this similarity sufficient to include any such society within the scope of this canon. They rely on the decree of the Sacred Congregation of the Holy Office of August 5, 1846, which states that "Secret societies mentioned in Pontifical Constitutions are understood all those which propose something against the Church or gov-

---

[36] Cerato, *Censurae Vigentes,* n. 55.

[37] Ayrinhac, *Penal Legislation,* n. 257.

[38] Canon 19.

[39] Quigley, J., *Condemned Societies* (Washington, 1927), p. 55.

[40] Sole, o. c., n. 361; Cipollini, o. c., n. 40; Noldin, H., *De Poenis Ecclesiasticis* (Innsbruck, 1921), n. 74.

ernment, whether or not they require an oath of secrecy." [41]  Others [42] require secrecy, Blat and Genicot sworn secrecy, and Blat an oath of blind obedience as well.  All agree that the *Carbonari*, specifically mentioned in the Constitution *"Apostolicae Sedis"* of Pius IX [43] and the Fenians, condemned by name and under censure in the decrees of the Holy Office of January 12, 1870,[44] as also all anarchistic, communistic, nihilistic, or terroristic associations are prohibited under penalty in this canon.  It is disputed as to whether or not socialism is included, but the answer would seem to require a distinction.  If it is merely a question of a political party professing the common doctrines of socialism and striving by legitimate means to acquire control of the government through parliamentary majorities, and if it is not constituted as an organic society, it certainly does not come under the meaning of this canon.[45]  If organized as a society and actively endeavoring to injure the Church or State it undoubtedly does fall under the censure of this canon.  Certain other societies also with obviously anti-Catholic, anti-religious, or anti-civil aims, provided they attempt by active means to attain their ends, would certainly be included, such as the Ku-Klux Klan, Katipunan Society, etc.  It is not so clear that societies whose aims and activities are rather academic, such as the biblical societies, neo-Protestants, Old Catholics, etc., are condemned under censure.  Some affirm [46] while others deny.[47]  The very fact of the dispute calls the law into doubt in their regard, and therefore renders it impossible to urge it on them.[48]

[41] *Fontes*, 899.

[42] Cerato, o. c., n. 55; Blat, *Comment.*, etc., *"De Delictis et Poenis,"* Vol. V, n. 177; Genicot, E., *Institutiones Theologiae Moralis* (Brussels, 1922), Vol. II, n. 94.

[43] *Fontes*, 552.

[44] S. C. S. Off., 12 January, 1870; Collectanea, S. Cong. de Prop. Fidei, Vol. II, n. 1350.

[45] Chelodi, *Jus Poenale*, n. 71; Genicot, *Institutiones*, II, n. 94.

[46] *V. g.*, Cipollini, *De Censuris*, n. 40; Sole, *De Delictis et Poenis*, n. 361.

[47] *V. g.*, Cerato, *Censurae Vigentes*, n. 55; Ayrinhac, *Penal Legislation*, n. 257.

[48] Canon 15.

Some we know are definitely excluded from this class, as those condemned societies mentioned specifically by the Holy Office in response to a query by the Second Plenary Council of Baltimore, *viz.*, Odd Fellows, Knights of Pythias, Sons of Temperance,[49] Independent Order of Good Templars.[50] These are forbidden under pain of grave sin, but not of censure. Others, such as the Young Men's Christian Association and Rotary Clubs, of which the Church has expressed disapproval, are not even expressly forbidden, at least by common law. The female societies such as the Eastern Star, Rebeccas and Pythian Sisters, connected with the condemned bodies are likewise forbidden and under the same penalties, whether of censure or only of sin, as the male societies.[51]

As regards the term "machinate" or "plot," the general opinion seems to be that unlawful activity, or the use of unlawful means is intended. Either the thing itself, as when it is against the Church, must be unlawful, even though the means adopted be according to legal procedure, or the means used must be illicit, though not necessarily violent, as when the state or government is attacked illegally. An organization which seeks by lawful means to change the form of government can scarcely be considered a reprobated society or "sect" akin to the Masons, Cipollini [52] and others to the contrary notwithstanding. One could hardly class the Fascists and Royalists of Spain, and the Monarchists of Austria, for instance, as "sects resembling the Masons."

Nor can it be pointed out quite definitely just what "legitimate civil power" may mean. It can hardly be said to signify simply the established order or *"de facto"* government. In the first place, it is not indisputable from reason or revelation to whom the sovereign power has been communicated by God. In the next place, it is rather disputable from the theology regarding prescription that a usurpatory

---

[49] S. C. S. Off., 20 August, 1894—*Fontes*, IV, p. 489, n. 117.

[50] S. C. S. Off., 9 August, 1893—*Fontes*, IV, p. 482, n. 1167. One must be careful not to confound the Good Templars with the Knights Templars. The latter are really Masons.

[51] Letter of Apostolic Delegation, Washington, No. 15352-C, 2 August, 1907. *Cf.* Fanning, W. H., "Societies, Secret," in *Catholic Encyclopedia*, XIV, p. 74.

[52] Cipollini, *De Censuris*, n. 40.

régime, vitiated in its root of acquisition, can ever obtain, even by prescription, a legitimate title. Furthermore, such régimes, for instance, as the Soviets in Russia or the Callesistas in Mexico, could evidently never attain either the rank of legitimate governments or the sanction of the Church no matter how long they might keep themselves in power. Nor can recognition by other nations or even the Holy See serve as a completely reliable norm, for recognition of a fact in no way guarantees the legitimacy of that fact. Hence, it may be concluded that as regards societies which plot against civil power, only those which are condemned by name or which from their nature are actively hostile to all legitimate civil power—nihilists, anarchists, and the like—can in practice be included under the law of this canon, for the uncertainty regarding others renders it inoperative in practice.

It should further be noted that these penalties concerning religious, *viz.,* privation of office and of active and passive voice, are *ferendae sententiae,* but mandatory; they are ordinarily incurred only when the general excommunication is incurred for the crime by the laity, and are in addition to this censure.

The obligation to denounce religious to the Holy Office is introduced for the first time by the Code. It obliges all who know of the offense, and is of itself a grave obligation, but it falls primarily upon superiors, pastors and ordinaries. It must be made, not through religious superiors, even in exempt institutes, as these are forbidden to interfere in matters pertaining to the Holy Office,[53] but either through the local ordinary or directly to the Holy Office.

[53] Canon 501, § 2.

## CHAPTER III

## THE VIOLATION OF THE CLOISTER[1]

### Canon 2342

Canon 2342 on the violation of the cloister falls under the scope of the present work in its second and third numbers. The first number does not pertain to religious exclusively nor does it contain a special penalty for religious, therefore, it is not included herein. The second number relates to the violation of the cloister of male regulars by women, applies in a particular way to religious superiors, and contains a special sanction against religious. The third number concerns exclusively a definite class of religious, namely, nuns who violate their cloister by unlawful egress.

### Article 1. Cloister of Male Regulars

### Canon 2342, n. 2°

**Canon 2342. Plectuntur ipso facto excommunicatione Sedi Apostolicae simpliciter reservata:**

**2° Mulieres violantes regularium virorum clausuram et superiores aliique, quicunque ii sint, eas cuiuscunque aetatis introducentes vel admittentes; et praeterea re-**

---

[1] The penal law concerning violations of the cloister was exhaustively treated by the Rev. V. T. Schaaf, O.F.M., J.C.D., in his dissertation on *The Cloister* presented to the faculty of Sacred Sciences at the Catholic University of America in 1921. There has been no new legislation or decision on this matter since that time, nor have any subsequent studies in any way altered the doctrine of that dissertation. Since therefore it remains the last word on this subject even today, the best thing that can be done here is to reproduce from it the points which pertain to the scope of this work. Outside research has yielded practically nothing not contained therein. *Cf.* also Ayrinhac, *Penal Legislation,* nn. 283-286; Sole, o. c., nn. 374, 375; Cappello, o. c., nn. 320-327; Cerato, o. c., nn. 60, 61; Cipollini, *op. cit.,* nn. 45-50; Chelodi, *Jus Poenale,* n. 77; Blat. Comment., *"De Delictus et Poenis,"* V, n. 183; Hollweck, o. c., § 158.

**ligiosi introducentes vel admittentes priventur officio,
si quod habeant, et voce activa ac passiva.***

The law concerning the cloister of male regulars is contained in
Canon 598, § 1, after the preceding canon has described the papal
cloister. Women of any age, class or condition, must not under any
pretext, be allowed to enter it, the only exception to this absolute
prohibition being for wives of the highest actual executive of the state
with their retinues, granted in the second paragraph of this canon.

The present Canon 2342, n. 2, prescribes the penalty for violation of this law, namely, excommunication incurred by the very act
of entering, and reserved simply to the Holy See, which penalty falls
not only on the women who enter, but on "superiors and others,
whomsoever they may be, who *introduce* or *admit* women of any
age whatsoever." The general excommunication incurred by women
who enter is outside the scope of this subject; whether or not that
incurred by "superiors and others" falls within it was not so clear
under the pre-Code law. Schaaf,[2] citing other authors,[3] states that
besides superiors only *regulars* who introduced or admitted women
incurred this penalty under the constitution of Pius IX. However,
the Constitution, *"Apostolicae Sedis"* itself [4] says explicitly, " . . . superiors and others admitting them." Under the Constitution, *"Ubi
Gratiae,"* of Gregory XIII,[5] only regulars who introduced them into

---

* Canon 2342. The following incur *ipso facto* excommunication reserved
*simpliciter* to the Holy See:

2° Women who violate the enclosure of male regulars, and Superiors and
others, whoever they may be, who introduce or admit women of any age whatsoever; besides, religious who introduce or admit them should be deprived of
their Office, if they hold any, and of active and passive voice.

[2] Schaaf, V. T., *The Cloister* (Cincinnati, 1921), pp. 90, 91.

[3] Pennachi, J., *Commentaria in Constitutionem Apostolicae Sedis* (Rome,
1883), I, 791; Mocchegiani, P., *Jurisprudentia Ecclesiastica ad usum et com-
moditatem utriusque cleri* (ad Clarus Aquas, 1904, 1905), I, 202; Piatus, F.,
*Commentarius in Constitutionem Apostolicae Sedis* (Tornaci, 1881), 181, 666.

[4] II, 7°—*Fontes*, n. 552; Pius V, in Constitution, *"Regularium,"* of October
24, 1566; *Fontes*, n. 115, § 4, pronounces the loss of office, active and passive
voice and suspension *a divinis* on regulars where guilty.

[5] *Fontes*, n. 147, § 3.

their own, not into another convent fell under the ban, nor did religious of simple vows or lay servants of the monastery.[6]

Today there is no longer any doubt. All persons guilty of the offense except Cardinals[7] and children below the age of puberty[8] incur the excommunication, whether or not they are religious or in any way connected with the house. This is clear from the last part of this number, where another penalty proper to religious is added, which alone falls within the scope of this subject. This penalty is deprivation of office, if they hold any, and of active and passive voice.

First, it should be noted that this additional penalty for religious is incurred for the identical offense for which all incur excommunication. This penalty, however, is *ferendae sententiae*, and hence, the subjective elements which might excuse from the *latae sententiae* censure[9] do not excuse from this vindictive penalty, though circumstances may bring about an alleviation or even cancellation of the penalty in virtue of Canon 2223, § 3, as explained above.[10]

The penalty is incurred by "introducing" or "admitting" women within the cloister. Concerning the precise meaning of these two terms there was much discussion. "Introducing" implied some positive coöperation, though in what degree was undecided, while only superiors, janitors, and those enjoined with the duty of guarding the cloister could "admit" outsiders, either positively by granting them entrance or negatively by not preventing it, when they were able and in duty bound to do so. Thus the common opinion[11] though some[12] included among those "admitting" even such as might come upon women in the cloister and fail to expel or attempt to expel them. This certainly is going too far under the existing jurisprudence in penal

---

[6] Schaaf, o. c., pp. 90, 91; Hollweck, § 158, footnote 5.

[7] Canon 2227, § 2.

[8] Canon 2230. The age of fourteen for boys and twelve for girls. Canon 88, § 2. Many hold the age to be fourteen for girls also. Their reasoning is not compelling.

[9] Canon 2229, § 3, n. 1°.

[10] Chap. II, Art. 1, footnote 10.

[11] Schaaf, o. c., p. 92.

[12] Cipollini, o. c., n. 47.

matters. After all, the discussion of word meanings is not so important as the question of what coöperation entails the penalties, which, as Schaaf rightly remarks, must be answered from Canons 2231 and 2209.[13] Canon 2231 pronounces against coöperators named in the first three paragraphs of Canon 2209 the same penalty as is incurred by the principal offender, while it excepts from such penalty those mentioned in the last four paragraphs of that canon. From these canons as premises, it may be concluded (1) that all who by common plan physically concur, or as Schaaf says, are "in collusion" with the intruder incur the penalties;[14] (2) so also, if from the nature of the crime an accomplice is necessary, all who act as such an accomplice and render aid without which the offense could not have been committed.[15] If the crime could have been committed even without such aid and with it was only made easier the penalty is not incurred,[16] unless there was collusion with the offender.[17] According to these norms it must be decided whether in a particular case merely opening the door or showing the way to the intruder entails the prescribed penalties. (3) Finally the penalties are incurred by those who command or commission a person to enter illicitly, or one prohibited to be permitted to enter, for he is the principal author of the crime.[18] Such a one would not incur, provided his command had not been efficacious, either because the violation would have taken place even without it [19] or had been retracted before the crime was committed, even though the culprits had persisted in their offense.[20] Those who by suggestion, counsel, or persuasion, induce a woman to enter or any one to admit or introduce her, incur only in case they are the cause of the violation, and have not retracted before the crime was committed.[21]

---

[13] Schaaf, o. c., n. 92.

[14] Canon 2209, § 1.

[15] Canon 2209, §§ 2 and 3.

[16] Canon 2209, § 4.

[17] Canon 2209, § 1; Schaaf, o. c., p. 93.

[18] Canon 2209, § 3.

[19] Canon 2209, §§ 3 and 4.

[20] Canon 2209, § 5.

[21] Canon 2209, §§ 3, 4 and 5.

According to the virtually unanimous opinion of almost all the authors, another class of coöperators fell under penalties, namely, superiors and others whose special duty it was to care for the enclosure, even if their coöperation consisted only in not preventing the violation when they were able and bound to do so. This obviously comes from the old definition given to the term "admit." As Schaaf rightly points out, it is to be accepted only under distinctions, according to the principles of penal laws contained in the Code and cited just above, as follows:

If the neglect on the part of one who is able to prevent the unlawful entrance of a woman amounts to permission to enter, either tacit or expressed, and thus be intended, he is guilty of coöperation by common consent,[22] and therefore incurs the penalties, whether or not his office entails custody of the cloister. If the neglect is not intended or necessarily to be construed as permission, as for instance, if a religious conversing at some distance from the entrance to the cloister sees a woman about to enter, and does not bother to stop her, though he could easily do so, he does not incur. There is no formal coöperation or complicity in the sense of Canon 2209, § § 1 and 3.[23]

As Schaaf correctly states, this applies also to superiors and others having charge of the cloister as regards the excommunication, but in view of § 6 of Canon 2209, which defines the guilt of those coöperating by neglecting their duty, and Canon 2231, requiring proportionate punishment for them, the privation at least of office, if not of active and passive voice, might well be inflicted on one so guilty.

That the problem is to be solved on the common grounds of coöperation in general, and not on any arbitrary meaning of the terms "introduce" or "admit" is conclusively proved by the author just cited. As he says, "admission" and "introduction" are ordinarily the only ways in which one can coöperate in the unlawful ingress, for either the woman enters by herself, or someone brings or lets her in. The disjunction seems quite complete. Moreover, the canon repeats the former law and retains the wording for two rea-

[22] Canon 2209, § 1.

[23] Schaaf, o. c., pp. 93, 94.

sons: First, lest by dropping the coöperators, they might be considered as no longer falling under censure; and Second, because it extends beyond the ordinary rules of coöperation, inasmuch as the woman brought in or let in may not herself be culpable at all, as will be seen below. Nevertheless, though in this sense those "admitting" and "introducing" are not mere coöperators, the example last given of the negligent religious who did not bother to prevent the violation of the cloister does not come under this head, and will not incur the excommunication. Evidently there is not in this case the "malice" required by Canon 2200 for constituting a crime; it is rather the *proxima dolo*, or "next thing to malice," described in Canon 2203 as being present when one neglects to take the ordinary means of avoiding a foreseen violation of the law. They do not "admit" or "introduce" according to the proper meaning of those words,[24] but at worst merely connive at the violation. Hence, whether "admitting" or "introducing" be considered as simple coöperation or as crimes in themselves, he who coöperates merely negatively in a woman's illicit entrance does not incur the censure,[25] though a religious may incur one or all of the penalties proper to religious.[26] In the case where the violation occurs through negligence of a superior, porter, or the like, but was not foreseen, not only the excommunication, but most likely even the special penalties for religious would not be incurred, though some punishment would be called for.

Some have held that those who come upon a woman, in the cloister, whether she entered in good faith or bad, and did not immediately put her out, at least if they be those charged with the custody of the cloister, incurred the penalties, and anyone who caused her to delay within the cloister likewise fell under censure. Others limited it to superiors, porters and the like. But if the words of the Code and principles of penal laws be followed, strictly, as they must be, neither of these opinions can be admitted today. There is no coöperation in the unlawful entrance, and even though the intruder be in bad faith, the crime is already fully committed and acts subse-

---

[24] Canon 2228.

[25] Schaaf, o. c., pp. 94, 95.

[26] Canons 2209, § 6, and 2231.

quent to it do not partake of the imputability of the crime committed.[27]   Moreover, "admit" here obviously means "permit to enter."   Now a penalty is only incurred when a crime is "complete in its kind according to the proper sense of the words of the law" [28] and those who tolerate her presence or even delay her exit do not in any sense permit her to enter, or admit her.   Nor can it be urged that the same or greater reason exists in this case, for it is not the offense punished by the law, which must receive strict interpretation [29] nor can the penalty be carried over to another case even though there is greater reason for it.[30]   The same must be said regarding the penalties proper to religious as the same principles apply, namely, that it is not the offense punished by law.   Other and severe punishments would be in order, but they are outside Canon 2342, § 2.   The penalties of the canon are incurred if one brings or lets a woman into the cloister, but once she is in there one can take her all through it and even to his own room without incurring them.   Of course, in all these cases the delinquents sin gravely, even though they escape the canonical penalties.

Under the former law there was some dispute as to whether or not one might admit an infant, or a girl below the age of puberty without incurring the penalties.   The argument used in support of the last and mildest opinion, namely that the girl must have attained the age of puberty before the penalty for admitting her was incurred, was that the penalty was inflicted on those admitting "them," that is, "women violating the cloister," and since those below the age of twelve were not excommunicated for violating it, they did not violate it and consequently those introducing or admitting them did not incur the excommunication either.[31]   This seems to have been straining the rules of logic too far and whatever its merits may have been, it has no place now.   Canon 2342, § 2, clearly states that excommunication and the other penalties are incurred for admitting women

---

[27] Canon 2209, § 7.

[28] Canon 2228.

[29] Canon 19.

[30] Canon 2219, § 3.

[31] Hollweck, o. c., § 152, footnote 2.

of any age whatsoever. The opinion of Blat [32] that the use of reason
is required in the child before the one admitting her is excommunicated, which opinion he states without attempting to prove and
which moreover directly contradicts the principles he himself lays
down in the same place, cannot be accepted. This canon is not
brought over integrally from the old law without important changes,
one of which concerns the wording on this very matter of age, and
consequently cannot be interpreted according to the commentators
on the former law,[33] but rather on the proper sense of its own words.[34]
This latter is clear, and takes no cognizance of the use of reason or
lack thereof on the part of the person admitted. The question of
the woman's imputability is not here at issue, and the penalties are
incurred for bringing in an infant child, a feeble-minded adult, or a
perfectly normal adult by violence, even though the woman herself
in all these cases is free from all fault. The same reason exists, all
are comprehended under the words of the law, there is no extending it from case to case or person to person, and the conclusion is inescapable.

The care of the cloister of regulars is in the hands of the regular
superiors in virtue of the privilege of exemption.[35] If these fail in
their duty, the local ordinary is bound to admonish them and should
this prove fruitless report the abuse to the Holy See.[36] Beyond this
he can do nothing on his own authority, unless the house be not
formal, hence under his special vigilance. In the latter case, if after
the warning there is no correction and the abuse becomes a scandal
to the people he can himself intervene to check it pending the action
of the Holy See.[37]

---

[32] Blat, *Commentarium*, V, "*De Delictis et Poenis*," n. 183.

[33] Canon 6, n. 2.

[34] Canons 6, n. 3, and 2228.

[35] Canon 615.

[36] Canon 617, § 1.

[37] Canon 617, § 2.

### Article 2. Cloister of Nuns

Canon 2342, n. 3°

**Canon 2342. Plectuntur ipso facto excommunicatione Sedi Apostolicae simpliciter reservata:**
**3°Moniales e clausura illegitime exeuntes contra praescriptum, Canon 601.***

The present law concerning the cloister of nuns is contained in Canons 600 to 603 inclusive, with the penal sanction in the canon now under consideration. The Instruction of the Sacred Congregation of Religious published since the Code [38] in no way changes either the law itself or its penal sanction.

The cloister was first imposed on nuns by common law in the Constitution, *"Periculoso,"* of Boniface VIII,[39] but it was not until the Council of Trent [40] that this cloister was enforced by penalty in the general law of the Church. The censure was renewed, as has been seen in the historical synopsis, by St. Pius V, in his two Constitutions, *"Circa Pastoralis"* and *"Decori,"* by Pius IX, in the Constitution, *"Apostolicae Sedis,"* and finally in this canon of the Code.

The first point to determine is just who are liable to this censure, and next, precisely how it is incurred.

As to the first, the canon says, "nuns." According to Canon 488, n. 7, nuns are defined as "religious women with solemn vows, or, unless it appears otherwise from the nature of the case or from the context, religious women whose vows are normally solemn, but which, by a disposition of the Holy See, are simple in certain regions," now from the nature of the case here those nuns who normally take solemn vows but by prescription of the Holy See here and now take

---

* Canon 2342. The following incur *ipso facto* excommunication reserved *simpliciter* to the Holy See.

3. Nuns who leave the enclosure unlawfully contrary to the prescription of Canon 601.

[38] S. C. de Rel., February 6, 1924—A. A. S., XVI (1924), 96.
[39] Cap un, *de statu regularium*, III, 16 in VI°.
[40] Conc. Trid., Sess. XXV, *de regularibus*, C. 5.

simple vows, are not included under this canon, for the simple reason that they are not bound to the papal cloister.[41]  Consequently, the nuns here spoken of are religious with solemn vows.  They, and they alone, are liable to the censure.  The view of Sole [42] that all those bound by the law of the cloister are liable, namely the temporarily professed, novices and postulants, cannot be admitted, inasmuch as they are in no sense "nuns" and in virtue of the strict interpretation required for penal laws by Canon 19 and the prohibition "to extend a penalty from one person to another" of Canon 2219, § 3, they certainly do not incur the excommunication.  Moreover, no penalty for violation on the part of the simply professed, novices, and postulants is contained in the Code, nor can the penalty fixed by the "pagella" for girl students who leave be applied here, as it too would be an extension of penalty from one person to another in violation of Canon 2219, § 3,[43] and furthermore could not by its very nature be applied to the simply professed who in virtue of their vows are bound to return.

The censure is incurred by the nuns if they leave the cloister (*clausura*).  The opinion of Cerato [44] that only by egress from the monastery do they fall under censure cannot be sustained.  Granting some weight to his historical argument and the more benign interpretation to be given penal laws [45] it still remains to be proven that the words monastery and cloister were not used synonymously in the papal documents.  Careful consideration of those documents seems to show that they were so used.  Further, not only a "milder" but first of all a strict interpretation must be given penal laws. The law says "cloister."  "Cloister" is defined in Canon 597.  Canon 601 forbids the nuns to leave their monastery except under certain

---

[41] S. C. Ep. et Reg. in *Parisien*, August 1, 1839, declared to be in force after the Code by the Pontiff.  Commiss. ad. C. C. Authentice Interpret, March 1, 1921, II, 2—A. A. S., XIII (1921), 178.

[42] Sole, o. c., n. 374; Cappello, whom Schaaf (pp. 143, 144) interprets as implying the same opinion in his earlier work, expressly holds the opposite in his 1925 and later edition, n. 323, 2.

43 Schaaf, o. c., p. 145, footnote 261, also p. 128.

[44] Cerato, o. c., n. 61b.

[45] Canon 2219, § 1.

conditions therein prescribed and somewhat amplified in a subsequent Instruction of the Sacred Congregation of Religious.[46]  The present canon excommunicates those who leave the "cloister" contrary to those prescriptions.  As Cerato himself admits, going into the Church or sacristy or up on the roof is forbidden under censure; also entrance into the parlor or other non-cloistered part of the house is a grave sin.  But the law makes no distinction in this matter between what is forbidden under censure or merely under grave sin; hence all grave sins in this matter carry excommunication with them.

The third point to consider is that the nun leaves unlawfully if she leaves contrary to what is prescribed in Canon 601, namely, without a special indult of the Holy See or on account of imminent danger of death or other very serious evil.  This evil may threaten a nun herself or the whole community because of the nun, as for instance insanity or affliction with a contagious disease.  In the latter case, the sufficiency of the reason must be recognized in writing by the local ordinary, if there is time.  A question arises as to whether this recognition by the ordinary is necessary for the validity of the permission to leave; in other words, whether one who had a legitimate reason, but neglected to have it recognized by the ordinary when she could have, would be excommunicated.  Blat denies it on the ground that the permission does not come from the ordinary [47] and therefore she does not act against the prescription of the canon. Schaaf [48] affirms it on the ground that she does act contrary to Canon 601.  This is true.  Were sufficiency of reason alone required, this canon would refer to the prescription of Canon 601, § 1. Instead it refers simply to Canon 601, apparently taking in everything prescribed there; consequently the strict interpretation necessary in this matter forces the acknowledgment of Schaaf's as the true response.

The unlawful egress herein contemplated is consummated the

---

[46] S. C. de Rel., 6, Feb., 1924—A. A. S., XVI (1924), 96.  English rendition in Woywod, S., *Canonical Decisions of the Holy See* (New York, 1933), Appendix IX.

[47] Blat, *Commentarium*, V, "*De Delictis et Poenis*," n. 183, 3.

[48] Schaaf, o. c., p. 146.

moment the entire body is entirely outside the limits of the cloister. Considering the strict interpretation to be given penal laws, lightness of matter can scarcely be admitted in these cases. The quantity or distance one has ventured outside the prescribed limits is not so much to be considered as the quality of malice or contempt which has led to the violation of so serious a law.

Finally it may be said that a nun lawfully outside her convent incurs no censure by leaving the house assigned as her residence, as this is not subject to the law of the cloister, though she may sin gravely; nor is she excommunicated for failing to return at the time set, for the penalty is prescribed for unlawful egress and cannot be extended to other cases. However, in virtue of Canon 603, she may be punished even with censures by the local ordinary and regular superior.

# CHAPTER IV

## FORGERY AND FALSIFICATION OF DOCUMENTS OF THE HOLY SEE

### Canon 2360, §§ 1 and 2

Canon 2360, § 1. Omnes fabricatores vel falsarii litterarum, decretorum vel rescriptorum Sedis Apostolicae vel iisdem litteris, decretis vel rescriptis scienter utentes incurrunt ipso facto in excommunicationem speciali modo Sedi Apostolicae reservatam.

§ 2. . . . religiosi [delictum de quo in § 1 commitentes] autem priventur omnibus officiis quae in religione habent et voce activa ac passiva, praeter alias poenis in propriis cuiusque constitutionibus statutas.*

THIS first canon of the title on the *Crimen Falsi* is the only one concerned with this crime which particularly affects religious, and this canon deals exclusively with the forgery or falsification of papal documents and use of such documents. Nevertheless, it will be necessary to examine the nature of the crime in general in order to deduce conclusions applicable to this particular form of falsity.

The *Crimen Falsi* in general may be defined as an alteration or suppression of truth done with malice, usually to the detriment of another or for one's own benefit.[1] Two of these elements, namely,

---

* Canon 2360, § 1. All forgers or falsifiers of letters, decrees or rescripts of the Apostolic See, or those knowingly using these same letters, decrees or rescripts incur *ipso facto* excommunication *speciali modo* reserved to the Holy See.

§ 2. . . . Moreover . . . religious guilty of this crime are to be deprived of whatever office they may have in their institute, and of active and passive voice, besides other penalties prescribed in their own constitutions.

[1] D'Annibale, *Commentarium in Constitutione, "Apostolicae Sedis,"* II, n. 78, in Sole, n. 410, with whose definition those of Ayrinhac, *Penal Legislation,* n. 320, Blat, *Comm.* V, n. 200; Chelodi, *Jus Poenale,* n. 776; Pruemmer, *Man. J. C.,* q. 599, R. 1, and others agree in substance.

the malice or intention of deceiving, and the perversion of truth are admitted by all as essential to the crime.  As to the third element, namely, that injury come or may come to another or advantage to one's self, there is some dispute.  The pre-Code authors all held that it was essential and some [2] still maintain it.  Others [3] follow Cappello in the view that the contempt for the Apostolic See inherent in any falsification of apostolic documents was sufficient to constitute the crime.  In this even some of the older writers [4] concurred on the ground that this was injury to the Holy See.  The latter opinion seems more sound in itself, especially in regard to the canon in hand, the text of which in no way implies that the intention of injuring anyone or benefitting one's self is required for the crime or to incur the punishment.  However, it would be difficult to enforce it, in the external forum at least, in as much as the dissent of such noted authors would put it in the class of doubtful penal laws which do not urge.[5]

Three distinct species of the crime of falsehood, relating to papal documents, are punished by this canon: forgery or fabrication, falsification, or use of forged or falsified documents.

Forgery or fabrication is the composition of an entire document, never published by the Holy See, and the affixing thereto of the papal seal, signature, etc., though as Ayrinhac says, the affixing of such seal and signature to an already existing document would be equivalent to forging it,[6] in as much as it thus acquires a false papal character.

Falsification is the alteration, addition, suppression, substitution of a document issued by the Holy See in such a way that the principal thing intended in issuing it is substantially changed.  Malicious fraud is postulated, and also deception or attempted deception in a serious

---

[2] Sole, o. c., n. 410; Chelodi, *Jus Poenale*, n. 77; Cipollini, o. c., n. 33.

[3] Cappello, o. c., n. 280, 6; Ayrinhac, *Penal Legislation*, n. 320, 1b; Cerato, o. c., p. 169.

[4] *V.g.*, Reiffenstuel, *op. cit.*, 1, V, T. 20, n. 1; Vermeersch-Creusen, *Epitome*, III, n. 562.

[5] Canon 15.

[6] Ayrinhac, *Penal Legislation*, n. 320b, though Cappello, o. c., no. 280, designates it falsification.

matter, to constitute the crime of falsification contemplated in this canon. All the authors agree thus far, and likewise concede that fabrication, falsification and use, when perpetrated merely as a joke do not constitute the crime under consideration.

It is likewise agreed that the publication or use of these forged or falsified documents is not required to become guilty of the crime and liable to the penalties, though some [7] hold that the forgery or mutilation of a document which is to be immediately destroyed would not render one liable to the penalties. Further, all agree that the crime must be perfect and consummated—not merely attempted. Thus, the fabrication of a document is not complete, and hence, does not render one liable to the punishment, till the forged signature and seals are affixed; nor the falsification unless the document itself be authentic and truly signed and sealed.[8]

In consequence of this it follows that it is only tampering with the original document, or drawing up a document purporting to be an original, or at the very most, an authentic legal copy that is forbidden under the penalties of this canon. Hence, distortion of announcements from the Vatican or from the Curia, as for example, erroneous translations and newspaper reports, or even false reports of apostolic pronouncements would not come under the offense punished by this canon, unless these copies, translations, etc., bore a legally authentic character.

As to the nature of the documents enumerated in the canon there is general agreement, with one or two dissenting voices. Letters, decrees, and rescripts of the Apostolic See are named specifically in the canon. According to Ayrinhac, Cappello and Cerato this designation includes all official documents issued by the Pope, exclusive of his private letters, or by the Roman congregations, tribunals, and offices;[9] not by Papal legates or lower authorities.[10] Other simply explain *letters* as including bulls, briefs, encyclicals, epistles, of the Pontiff; *decrees* as documents stating what it is to be believed or done

---

[7] Cerato, o. c., p. 169; Cipollini, o. c., n. 33; Sole, o. c., n. 410.

[8] Cipollini, o. c., n. 33.

[9] Canon 7.

[10] Ayrinhac, *Penal Legislation*, n. 320b; Cerato, *Censurae Vigentes*, p. 168d; Cappello, *De Censuris*, n. 281.

in matters of faith, morals or discipline, under a proper sanction;[11] and *rescripts* as the response to petitions made in writing, whether these define a right or grant a favor, whether given in gratuitous or commissory form.

Blat [12] interprets the term more strictly, limiting letters to "Apostolic Letters properly so called," that is, those given "in the form of bull, brief, encyclical or Pontifical epistles undersigned by the secretary." He bases this on the interpretation of the old law and Canon 19, which demands strict interpretation in penal laws. This opinion cannot be sustained for the simple reason that the term, Apostolic Letter, has no fixed and rigid signification, and is commonly used as widely and loosely as the common interpretation of this canon would have it.[13]

Furthermore, even should the term "Apostolic Letter" be narrowed to mean only those Papal documents mentioned in Canon 2318, § 1, it would not be legitimate to conclude that this term is synonymous with "letters of the Apostolic See" mentioned in the present canon, as the term "Apostolic See" is expressly interpreted by Canon 7 to include not only the Pope but all the congregations, tribunals and offices of the Roman Curia.

As said above the mere composition of these false documents renders the offender liable to the penalties even though no use is made of them, but when use is made of them another crime, punished by this canon, is committed. Knowing use of documents forged or falsified by another party likewise incurs the same penalties. In neither case is it necessary that the object sought through the use of the documents be attained; use alone, that is the presentation or exhibition of them, constitutes the offense. The use must be made with knowledge that the document was forged or falsified; otherwise, good faith will excuse, but this good faith must be proved; it is not presumed. Moreover, though crass or supine ignorance will excuse a person from the *latae sententiae* excommunication [14] it does not ex-

---

[11] Cipollini, *De Censuris*, n. 33.

[12] Blat, *Commentarium*, V, n. 201.

[13] *Cf.* Cicognani, *Canon Law*, p. 83.

[14] Canon 2229, § 2.

cuse religious from the *ferendae sententiae* penalties of this canon, namely, loss of any office they may hold, and of active and passive voice.  These penalties are preceptive and thus subject to what was said above at the end of Article 1 of Chapter II.

Coöperators are not mentioned here and consequently the general norms of Canons 2231 and 2209, explained above in the first article of the previous chapter, apply here.

These punishments are stated in this canon as additional to other penalties set down in the particular constitutions of each institute. These constitutional penalties will probably not be directed against this specific crime, but most likely concern falsehood in general. This canon states that the penalties it contains do not abrogate the constitutional penalties, and that both are to be inflicted upon the guilty party.

The crime is not common, at least in our day, and especially among religious.  Like the penalty against violation of the seal of confession—a crime most rarely, if ever, committed—it is rather the gravity of the offense than the danger of its commission which causes it to be mentioned here with such important sanctions.

# CHAPTER V

## CONTUMACIOUS NEGLECT OF DIOCESAN CONFERENCES

### Canon 2377

**Canon 2377. Sacerdotes contra praescriptum Canon 131, § 1, contumaces, Ordinarius pro suo prudenti arbitrio puniat; quod si fuerint religiosi confessarii curam animarum non gerentes, eos ab audiendis saecularium confessionibus suspendat.***

Canon 131, § 1, prescribes that several times a year on days determined by the ordinary meetings shall be held in the episcopal city and each deanery for the discussion of moral and liturgical matters, to which the ordinary may add whatever exercises he judges opportune for the promotion of science and piety of the clergy. These meetings are called conferences or collations. The second paragraph of the canon states that if it be found difficult to hold these meetings the ordinary may substitute the written solution of questions to be sent to him.

The third paragraph enumerates those on whom the obligation of either attending the meetings or submitting the solutions falls. They are all secular priests, as well as all religious, even exempt, who have charge of souls,[1] unless they have obtained an express exemption from the ordinary beforehand; likewise all religious, including ex-

---

* Canon 2377. The Ordinary shall punish according to his own prudent judgment priests who are contumacious against the prescription of Canon 131, § 1; but if they are religious confessors not having charge of souls they are to be suspended from hearing the confessions of seculars.

[1] Those having charge of souls (*curam animarum habentes*) means not only pastors but also religious who act as curates or assistants in a parish, and even chaplains to hospitals or other pious houses provided they act for and assist the pastor in all branches of the parochial ministry. Catechists are not included, apparently because they help in only one, not every branch of the ministry. Pont. Com., 12 February, 1935—A. A. S., XXVII (1935), 92. *Cf. Irish Ecclesiastical Record*, May, 1935, pp. 532, 533.

empt, who have obtained faculties to hear confessions from the ordinary, unless conferences are held in their own houses.

This present Canon, 2377, imposes on the ordinary the right and duty to punish, not those who fail to fulfill the obligation, but those who are contumacious against it, that is, who persist in neglect of it even after due warning has been given them.[2]  The penalty for religious having care of souls, as for all secular priests, is undetermined but preceptive, as is evident from the use of the jussive subjunctive.[3]  The ordinary must inflict punishment, but its kind and quality is left to his own judgment.  In the case of religious who have not the care of souls but have faculties from him the punishment is not only preceptive but determined, and the only discretion he has in the matter is that given by Canon 2223, § 3.[4]  The faculties for hearing the confessions of seculars are to be suspended.  As Blat remarks [5] this evidently constitutes a grave cause required by the Code [6] for suspending a priest's faculties to hear confessions.  In all this no distinction is made between exempt and non-exempt religious, but it is plain that notwithstanding this suspension by the local ordinary the former retain the faculties to hear confessions within the order that they have from their own ordinaries.[7]

Ayrinhac states that the penalty of this canon applies also to those who obstinately neglect to submit the answers to the assigned questions in writing, that is, are contumacious against the prescriptions of Canon 131, § 2.[8]

Although it seems reasonable that this should be so, and there exists the same reason for its being so, it cannot be admitted in virtue of the principles of penal law laid down in the Code.  Laws which prescribe a penalty must be strictly interpreted [9] and no penalty can

---

[2] Canon 2333, § 2.  *Cf.* also Sole, o. c., n. 438; Ayrinhac, *Penal Legislation,* n. 347, 2.

[3] Blat, *Commentarium,* V, n. 220.

[4] *Ibid, l. c.*

[5] *Ibid., l. c.*

[6] Canon 880, § 1.

[7] Canons 875, § 1, and 514, § 1.

[8] Ayrinhac, *Penal Legislaiton,* n. 347, 2.

[9] Canon 19.

be carried from one case to another.[10]   Canon 2377 expressly punishes those who are contumacious against the prescription of Canon 131, § 1, and only they are liable to the penalties, for while it is true there is no *prescription* in § 2, if the penalty were to apply to its provision there would be no point in specifying § 1.

[10] Canon 2219, § 3.

## CHAPTER VI

## COMMERCIAL TRADING

### Canon 2380

**Canon 2380. Clerici vel religiosi mercaturam vel negotiationem per se aut per alios exercentes contra praescriptum, Canon 142, congruis poenis pro gravitate culpae ab Ordinario coerceantur.***

THE prohibition against commercial trading in Canon 142 is directed only to clerics, but it is expressly extended to religious by Canon 592. The present canon contains the penalty against both clerics and religious. As is apparent, from the text of the canon, *mercaturam vel negotiationem,* not merely trading in the strict sense, but business or commercial ventures in general, are forbidden.

Trading in the strict sense is the habitual buying and selling for the sake of gain [1] or the buying of a thing that it may be sold unchanged for a higher price.[2] Thus four things are required: (1) buying, for if the thing be already had or is the produce of one's own land or animals, it is not trading. (2) Buying in order to sell, which is designated political trading, as distinct from domestic or economic trading which is the buying for one's own use and sale of the superfluous even though at profit.[3] (3) Selling at a higher price, for selling at no profit or a loss to friends or the poor is not trading in the legal sense. (4) Finally, the thing must be unchanged, for if by one's own industry the thing is improved the idea of lucrative trading ceases. If, however, the work of improvement is done by hired help it remains

---

* Canon 2380. Clerics or religious carrying on trade or commerce personally or through others against the prescription of Canon 142 are to be coerced by the Ordinary with penalties befitting the gravity of their fault.

[1] Ayrinhac, *Penal Legislation,* n. 350, 1°.

[2] St. Alphonsus III, 836; Sole, n. 441.

[3] Blat, *Commentarium textus Codicis Juris Canonici,* Vol. II, "*De Personis,*" n. 81; Sole, o. c., n. 441; Chelodi, *Jus Poenale,* n. 97, 5, all concede economic trading to be permitted to religious. No dissenters from this opinion have come to hand.

lucrative trading, for as Blat [4] says then both the work and the object have been purchased for sale with profit. All agree that this is forbidden by the canons. Even though it be not trading properly so called it is strictly commercial activity.

This trading is forbidden to clerics and religious whether it is done by themselves or through others, for themselves or for others, even, consequently, by officials of a religious community for the benefit of the community. As is seen from the definition as explained above the maintenance of a farm and sale of its products for the sustenance of the community is not commercial trading; neither is the sale of vestments, paintings, and such handiwork of the members of the community. The sale of such religious articles as statutes, pictures, books, rosaries, etc., bought wholesale to be resold, if profit be made thereby, certainly does seem to fall under the forbidden trading, though the sale of books, periodicals and pamphlets which are the work of members of the community does not.

Vermeersch would permit religious to sell at profit books, banners of societies and religious articles in general, provided the profit be used for pious purposes, and especially if the bishop expressly or tacitly permits it, on these grounds: (1) by buying wholesale and taking care of the articles for sale they perform a personal work and take a risk, for which the profit is a reward; (2) by buying wholesale they get the goods at a lower price and they can keep their savings; and moreover, by such purchase they eliminate the inconvenience that each would experience should each one be forced to buy for himself; (3) in the price of a thing, the honest remuneration of labor as well as the interest on the money spent and the danger of loss may be computed. Hence, the labor, risk of loss from things not sold, and interest on the money with which the goods were bought, are compensated for by this profit.[5]

This reasoning seems more specious than sound and if the principles set forth were followed to their logical conclusion, any honest business negotiation or commercial enterprise would be licit for clerics and religious and these canons would be a dead letter.

[4] Blat, *Commentarium*, II, n. 81.

[5] Vermeersch, "De Negotiatione Clericorum," *Periodica*, XXII (1933), 210*-211*.

Some concessions, however, may be made. Buying and selling at some profit would not seem to bear the stigma of forbidden negotiations provided the profit were used merely to cover running expenses and the things were kept and sold merely for the convenience of others, as some devotional articles at certain shrines. However, when this is engaged in to such an extent that it becomes a commercial enterprise in competition with secular firms it certainly falls under the prohibition. Vromant allows a cleric to sell at the regular price what he has gotten at a lower price, on the ground that the profit is a gift from the first seller, but he expressly states that it is not lawful if the reason for the lower price was that he bought wholesale to sell each at a higher price.[6] This seems to cover the case very well. Ayrinhac [7] states that clerics, and so also religious in the name of the community, are permitted to lend money at the usual rate of interest and buy shares, stocks or bonds in industrial or commercial enterprises, provided this be done as an investment for the sake of dividends, not as speculation. This does not seem clear, at least in regard to commercial enterprises, for it seems very much like engaging in commerce through others. Thus Chelodi, who states it is illicit in regard to commercial enterprises and doubtful in regard to industrial.[8]

The penalties are *ferendae sententiae,* indefinite, and left to the discretion of the ordinary who is to inflict penalties befitting the gravity of the fault, taking all the circumstances into consideration. These penalties may be censures or vindictive penalties of greater or less gravity according to the gravity of the crime. They cannot be inflicted for one or two offenses for according to the definition of trading a habit is required.[9]

The ordinary here spoken of is the major superior for exempt clerical religious, the local ordinary for others.[10]

---

[6] Vromant, "De Negotiatione Clericis et Religiosis Interdicta," in *Jus Pontificium* IX (1929), 35.

[7] Ayrinhac, *Penal Legislation,* n. 350, 10.

[8] Chelodi, *Jus Poenale,* n. 97, 5.

[9] Chelodi, *Jus Poenale,* n. 97, 5; Ayrinhac, *Penal Legislation,* n. 350, 10.

[10] Canons 198 and 619.

## CHAPTER VII

# PENALTIES AGAINST DISMISSED RELIGIOUS CLERICS
## Canons 648, 669, § 2, 670, 671

In concluding this section regarding penalties for crimes committed against the general law of the Church it seems necessary to set forth certain definite penalties affecting a very definite class of religious for general and undetermined offenses.

With the exception of the crimes of apostasy from the Catholic Faith, flight with a person of the opposite sex, and attempting or contracting marriage, which are punished *ipso facto* by dismissal [1] the Code nowhere specifies what offenses are to be punished with dismissal. It does, however, presuppose that certain grievous crimes are so to be punished and when the religious guilty of them happens to be a cleric it inflicts on him in addition certain punishments proper to clerics. The disabilities for obtaining certain offices or exercising certain functions [2] are not, properly speaking, penalties, as they are incurred even by persons guilty of no offense who have lawfully obtained an indult of secularization. On the other hand no penalties strictly so called are inflicted on lay religious beyond the dismissal itself and whatever may be contained in the common law against any perpetrator of the offense.

The first of these penalties is found in Canon 648, which deals with dismissed religious with temporary vows:

> **Religiosus dimissus ad normam Canon 647 ipso facto solvitur ob omnibus votis religiosis, salvis oneribus ordini majori adnexis, si sit in sacris, et firmo praescripto Canon 641, § 1; 642; clericus autem in minoribus ordinibus constitutus eo ipso redactus est in statum laicalem.***

---

[1] Canon 646, § 1.
[2] Canon 642.

*Canon 648. The religious dismissed according to the terms of Canon 647 is *ipso facto* freed from all his religious vows, without prejudice to the obliga-

This reduction to the lay state may or may not be a penalty [3] according as the dismissal was in punishment of a crime or for other grave causes, not crimes, properly so called, but sufficient to warrant dismissal.[4] Whether a penalty or not it carries with it the loss of all offices, benefices, and the clerical rights and privileges [5] and those thus dismissed are forbidden to wear the ecclesiastical habit and tonsure.[6]

The penalty for those of perpetual vows is contained in Canon 669, § 2:

> **Professus qui vota perpetua emisit . . . a religione dimissus. . . . Si clericus est in minoribus ordinibus constitutus, eo ipso reducitur ad statum laicalem.****

It is precisely the same as for those of temporary vows, except that here it is always a penalty in punishment for the crimes which have brought about the dismissal.[7] In both cases the reduction is *ipso facto*, not on the commission of the crime, but on the effective execution of the dismissal.

When the religious is a cleric in sacred orders and the offense for which he was dismissed was a major offense, Canon 670 applies:

> **Clericus in sacris qui aliquod delictum commisit de quo in Canon 646, aut dimissus est ob delictum quod jure**

tions attached to major orders, if he has received them, and safeguarding the prescriptions of Canons 641, § 1, and 642; the cleric, however, who is in minor orders is reduced by such dismissal to the lay state. (Authorised English translation.)

---

[3] *Cf.* Canon 211.

[4] *Cf.* Canons 647, § 2, and 211, § 2.

[5] Canons 118-122.

[6] Canon 213.

** Canon 669, § 2. The religious who has made profession of perpetual vows and who has been dismissed from the Institute. . . . If he be a cleric and in minor orders, he is by the fact of dismissal reduced to the lay state. (Authorised English translation.)

[7] Canons 646, 649, 653, 654, 668.

**communi punitur infamia iuris vel depositione vel degradatione, perpetuo prohibetur deferre habitum ecclesiasticum.*****

The crimes mentioned in Canon 646 are apostasy from the Catholic Faith,[8] flight with a person of the opposite sex [9] and attempting or contracting marriage,[10] all of which carry *ipso facto* dismissal.

Those punished by common law with *ipso facto* infamy of law are:

(a) Apostates, heretics and schismatics who join a non-Catholic organization whether Christian or non-Christian, or simply belong to it without formal incorporation (Canon 2314, § 1, n. 3).

(b) Those who cast away the Sacred Species or carry off or retain Them for an evil purpose (Canon 2320).

(c) Those who violate the bodies or graves of the dead with a view to theft or any other evil purpose (Canon 2328).

(d) Those who lay violent hands on the person of the Pope, cardinals, or Papal legates (Canon 2343, § 1, n. 2; § 2, n. 2).

(e) The principals and seconds in duels (Canon 2351, § 2).

(f) Those guilty of bigamy, that is, those who are already validly married and attempt another marriage, even though by mere civil ceremony (Canon 2356).

(g) Lay persons lawfully condemned for crimes against the sixth commandment with minors under sixteen years of age, or for rape, sodomy, incest, or traffic in vice (Canon 2357, § 1).

The crimes mention under (f) and (g) do not come under this canon as they cannot apply to clerics.

The following are to be declared to have incurred infamy of law:

(a) Apostates from the Christian faith and all heretics and schismatics, although not enrolled in or belonging to a non-Catholic

---

*** Canon 670. A cleric in sacred orders who has committed any crime mentioned in Canon 646, or has been dismissed on account of a crime which is punished by common law with infamy of law or deposition or degradation, is perpetually forbidden to wear the ecclesiastical habit.

[8] *Cf.* supra, Part II, Chapter I.

[9] Infra, Part II, Chapter VIII, Article 3.

[10] Infra, Part II, Chapter X, Article 3.

sect unless they repent after having been admonished (Canon 2314, § 1, n. 2).

(b) Clerics in sacred orders whether secular or religious, who have committed a crime against the sixth commandment of the decalogue with minors under sixteen years of age, or been guilty of adultery, rape, bestiality, sodomy, traffic in vice, or incest with blood relatives or relatives by marriage within the first degree (Canon 2359, § 2).

The crimes punished by common law with deposition are:

(a) Apostasy from the Christian faith, heresy and schism if the culprit does not repent after a repeated admonition (Canon 2314, § 1, n. 2).

(b) Casting away the Sacred Species or carrying Them off or retaining Them for an evil purpose (Canon 2320).

(c) Pretending to celebrate Mass or hear confessions on the part of those who are not priests (Canon 2322, n. 1).

(d) Violation of the bodies or graves of the dead with a view to theft or any other evil purpose (Canon 2328).

(e) Effective procuration of abortion (Canon 2350, § 1).

(f) Commission of homicide, rape of a person of either sex below the age of puberty, sale of a man into slavery or for any other evil purpose, usury, robbery, theft whether qualified by aggravating circumstances changing the species of the sin, as for instance, sacrilegious theft of sacred things, or even ordinary theft in very notable matter, incendiarism or malicious and very notable destruction of things, grave mutilation, wounding, or violence (Canon 2354, § 1).

(g) Commission of a sin against the sixth commandment with minors under sixteen years of age, or adultery, rape, bestiality, sodomy, traffic in vice, incest with blood relatives or relatives by marriage within the first degree (Canon 2359, § 2).

(h) Notoriously passing to a kind of life alien to the clerical state by those in sacred orders if, warned a second time after three months have elapsed since the first warning, they do not repent (Canon 2379).

(i) Occupation of a benefice, office, or ecclesiastical dignity on one's own authority, or entering into the possession, government or administration of the same by one elected, presented, or nominated to it before he has received the necessary letters of confirmation or institution and shown them to those to whom he rightfully should, and refused to retire from the occupation, government or administration of the same office, benefice or dignity immediately upon being warned (Canon 2394, n. 2).

(j) Stubborn persistence in an office, benefice or dignity notwithstanding legitimate privation or removal, or illegitimate delay in withdrawing, in order to retain possession of it (Canon 2401).

The penalty of degradation may be inflicted on clerics:

(a) If already deposed and deprived of the ecclesiastical habit they continue for a year to give grave scandal (Canon 2305, § 2).

(b) If they give their names or publicly adhere to a non-Catholic sect, after fruitless admonition (Canon 2314, § 1, n. 3).

(c) If they lay violent hands on the person of the Roman Pontiff (Canon 2343, § 1, n. 3).

(d) If they are guilty of culpable homicide (Canon 2354, § 2).

(e) If they commit a specially grave crime of solicitation (Canon 2368, § 1).

(f) If those in sacred orders presume to contract marriage, even merely civilly, and being admonished do not repent within the time stated by the ordinary.

The above lengthy list is an elenchus of all the crimes punishable under Canon 670. The religious guilty of any one of these crimes and dismissed therefor from religion, even though not yet punished with infamy, deposition or degradation, is by the very fact of the dismissal [11] deprived of the ecclesiastical habit, secular and religious, a particular vindictive penalty for clerics [12] and carries with it the loss of all clerical privileges [13] and the charitable means of sustenance the ordinary is directed to give in case of necessity [14] to deposed clerics.

---

[11] Palombo, *De Dimissione Religiosorum,* p. 246.

[12] Canon 2298, n. 11.

[13] Canon 2304, § 2.

[14] Canon 2303, § 2.

Si vero dimittatur ob delicta minora iis de quibus in Canon 670:

1° Ipso facto suspensus manet, donec a Sancta Sede absolutionem obtinuerit.

2° Sacra Congregatio, si id expedire judicaverit, dimisso praecipiat ut, habitu cleri saeculari indutus commoretur in certa diocesi, indicatis Ordinario causis ob quas dimissus fuit.

3° Si dimissus praecepto de quo in n. 2, non paruerit, religio ad nihil tenetur, et dimissus eo ipso privatus est jure deferendi habitum ecclesiasticum.

4° Ordinarius dioecesis pro ejus commoratione designatae, religiosum in domum poenitentiae mittat vel eum committat curae ac vigilantiae pii ac prudentis sacerdotis; et si religiosus non paruerit servetur praescriptum n. 3.

6° Si dimissus vitae rationem ecclesiastico viro dignam non agat, transacto anno aut etiam prius, iudicio Ordinarii, privetur caritativo subsidio, ejiciatur e domo poenitentiae eique auferetur ius deferendi habitum ecclesiasticum ab ipso Ordinario, qui statim mittere curet opportunam relationem tum ad Sedem Apostolicam tum ad religionem.

If the crime for which the religious was dismissed should be less than those just enumerated he nevertheless incurs the following penalties contained in Canon 671:

1° *Ipso facto* suspension reserved to the Holy See. Obviously enough this is a censure as is plain from the use of the term absolution from it right here, and from explicit reference to it as such below in no. 7.

2° The Sacred Congregation may command that the dismissed religious live clothed as a secular cleric in a certain diocese whose ordinary is to be informed of the cause of his dismissal. This is one of the vindictive penalties proper to clerics.[15]

---

[15] Canon 2298, n. 7.

3°  If he refuses to fulfill this precept he is by that fact deprived of the ecclesiastical habit and the institute freed from all obligation of caring for him.

4°  If he accepts, however, he is to be sent by the local ordinary to a house of penance or commits him to the care and vigilance [16] of a pious and prudent priest, and if he refuses this the same penalty as for refusal to live in the diocese will be inflicted.

6°  Again, if he does not in the judgment of the ordinary act in a way becoming an ecclesiastical person he is, after a year's time or even earlier, to be deprived of the charitable subsidy and of the ecclesiastical habit by the ordinary, expelled from the house of penance, and an account of it sent immediately by the bishop to the Holy See, and to the institute.

[16] A penal remedy.  *Cf*. Canon 2311.

## SECTION II

## CRIMES AGAINST THE RELIGIOUS STATE

### CHAPTER VIII
### UNLAWFUL DEPARTURE FROM RELIGION

ARTICLE 1. APOSTASY.  CANON 2385

**Canon 2385.  Firmo praescripto Canon 646, religiosus apostata a religione, ipso iure incurrit in excommunicationem proprio Superiori maiori vel, si religio sit laicalis aut non exempta, Ordinario loci in quo commoratur, reservatam, ab actibus legitimis ecclesiasticis est exclusus, privilegiis omnibus suae religionis privatus; et si redierit, perpetuo caret voce activa et passiva, ac praeterea aliis poenis pro gravitate culpae a superioribus puniri debet ad normam constitutionum.***

THE oldest penal laws enacted against religious were in punishment of the crime of apostasy or desertion from religion.  As has been seen in the historical development of this subject, the penalty against unlawful abandonment of the religious life is almost as old as religious life itself; and is one of the two crimes against which the most penalties were enacted by the early councils.  An excommunica-

---

* Canon 2385.  Without prejudice to the prescription of Canon 646, the religious who has apostatized from his Institute incurs by the law itself (*ipso jure*) excommunication reserved to his own higher Superior or, in the case of a lay or non-exempt Institute, to the Ordinary of the place in which he resides; he is excluded from all legitimate ecclesiastical acts, deprived of all the privileges of his Institute; and, if he returns to it, he remains forever without active and passive voice, and, besides, he must be punished by his Superiors with other penalties according to the gravity of the fault, conformably to the Constitutions. (Authorised English Translation.)

tion *latae sententiae* of Boniface VIII [1] together with suspension and other penalties enacted later, perdured according to the common opinion [2] even after the Constitution, *"Apostolicae Sedis,"* down to the Code itself. These, however, only affected regulars, not religious of simple vows.

In the Decree of the Sacred Congregation of Religious of May 16, 1911, mentioned in Part I of this work, and in the schemata of the Code apostasy on the part of any religious was one of the crimes punished with *ipso facto* dismissal.

An apostate is defined by the Code as "one who, having made profession of perpetual vows, whether solemn or simple, unlawfully leaves the religious house with the intention of not returning, or who, with the intention of withdrawing himself from religious obedience, though he has lawfully left the house, does not return to it." [3] Obviously this includes all religious who have made final profession or perpetual vows, not those who have made profession of temporary vows. The nature of the institute, whether it be an order or congregation, or whether it be pontifical or diocesan, makes no difference, so long as the vows are perpetual. Women are included as well as men, [4] the opinion of certain authors [5] to the contrary notwithstanding. [6]

It seems hardly necessary to refute the isolated opinion of Cerato and Cipollini when confronted with the overwhelming authority of

---

[1] C. 2, *de Clerici vel Monachi saecularibus negotiis se immisceant*, III, 24 in VI°.

[2] Piat, F. Montensi, *Praelectiones Juris Regularis* (Tonnaci, 1906), 3rd ed., Vol. I, n. 219.

[3] Canon 644, § 1. (Authorized English Translation.)

[4] Canon 490.

[5] Cerato, *Censurae Vigentes*, p. 103; Cipollini, *De Censuris*, n. 81.

[6] Thus the common opinion, explicitly set forth by Ayrinhac, *Penal Legislation*, n. 357; Sole, o. c., n. 445 (p. 384, footnote 3); Chelodi, *Jus Poenale*, n. 101; Cappello, *De Censuris*, n. 389, 2 (p. 339, footnote 67); Pruemmer, D., *Manuale Juris Canonici* (Friburg, 1927), ed. 4th and 5th, q. 255. Implicitly also by those who make no distinction between male and female religious as Blat, o. c., V, *"De Delictis et Poenis,"* n. 228; II, *"De Personis,"* n. 723; Schäfer, *De Religiosis*, n. 564-571; Fanfani, *De Jure Rel.*, n. 491-494; Vermeersch-Creusen, *Epitome*, 5th ed., Vol. I, Part 2, nn. 803, 804; 4th ed., Vol. III, n. 589, etc.

the other authors, and in fact Cappello is the only one who takes issue with it. The opinion of Cerato is based first on the reservation to the major superior and the purely arbitrary restriction of the term, "lay institute," to congregations of men, as opposed to clerical institutes; and, secondly, on the allegation that nuns are punished elsewhere, by Canon 2342, § 3. As Cappello [7] points out, the crime punished in that canon is not apostasy nor even flight, but mere illicit egress from the cloister, and sisters are not affected by it at all. Furthermore, the limitation of "lay institutes" to those of men is wholly gratuitous and without foundation in law; it clearly violates the principle that "where the law does not distinguish neither ought we distinguish," and is patently contrary to the mandatory strict interpretation of penal laws.[8] Considering all this the conclusion of Cipollini [9] that "Practically, therefore, this censure, since it is at least doubtful, does not affect nuns and sisters," cannot be admitted. As he admits, the arguments in favor of the exception are very flimsy; they are easily refuted from the principles of law, and the authority of these two authors as against all the others does not suffice to make the penalty doubtful. In fact, their opinion must be said to lack all probability, both intrinsic and extrinsic, and the censure be held as certainly affecting all religious of perpetual vows, men and women.

The prescription of Canon 646 refers to those who flee with a person of the opposite sex, and will be dealt with in the third article of this chapter. They are, of course, included here if they do not intend to return; the present article concerns only simple apostasy.

This crime, as has been seen, requires, 1° perpetual profession; 2° departure from the religious house without permission, or the unlawful refusal to return even if departure has been licit; 3° the intention of not returning, that is, of withdrawing one's self from religious obedience. Consequently, the crime is composed of two elements—the *fact*, namely, of illicit departure from or remaining outside the house, and the *intention* of not returning or withdrawing one's self from religious obedience.

---

[7] Cappello, o. c., n. 389, 2.

[8] Canon 19.

[9] Cipollini, o. c., n. 81.

The *fact* can ordinarily be established without difficulty; the *intention* must be deduced in the external forum either from evident signs or from legal presumptions. Such signs would be attempted marriage, flight with one of opposite sex, assumption of laymen's duties, particularly military or political, etc.

When none of these signs are apparent, recourse must be had to legal presumption, the ground for which is laid down in the law itself: "The perverse intention referred to in § 1 is legally presumed when the religious within a month has neither returned nor manifested to his superior his intention of returning."[10] The month is to be computed from the day on which the religious ought to have returned, but the presumption herein established is *presumptio juris* only,[11] and therefore admits of both direct and indirect proof to the contrary.[12] It should be noted, however, that mere notification of the intention to return may itself be nullified by proof of insincerity, that is, by evidence that the intention is really lacking when return is easily possible and no serious attempt has been made to effect it.

The crime must be consummated before the penalties are incurred, and thus the two elements of fact and intention must be joined. Hence, one lawfully outside the house who forms the intention of not returning, but changes his mind and returns at the appointed time, is not subject to the penalties. On the contrary, one who leaves illicitly with this intention, though he may immediately repent of it and return does seem to incur, in the internal forum. The argument of Cappello[13] and Vermeersch-Creusen[14] that external manifestation is necessary for the consummation of the crime and, consequently, for the incurring of the penalties is certainly valid for the external forum. However, it does not seem to hold for the internal forum, as the latter authors seem to admit, for the censures are incurred *latae sententiae*, by the very fact of the crime, and no manifestation or proof is necessary. This was even the more com-

---

[10] Canon 644, § 2.

[11] Blat, *Comment.*, "De Personis," II, 723; Cappello, *De Censuris*, n. 389, 2; Chelodi, *Jus Poenale*, n. 101; Vermeersch-Creusen, *Epitome*, 1, 2, n. 804.

[12] Canon 1826.

[13] Cappello, o. c., n. 389, § 2.

[14] Vermeersch-Creusen, *Epitome*, III, 589.

mon opinion under the old law and the same reasons are still valid.[15]

The penalties incurred by apostates are, first of all, excommunication [16] with the inseparable effects which follow it,[17] the right to absolve from which is reserved to his own major superior in clerical exempt institutes, that is, the general or provincial, their vicars and all who have powers equivalent to those of provincials [18] in those institutes the majority of whose members receive the order of priesthood [19] and which are by law [20] or special privilege [21] exempt from the jurisdiction of the local ordinary.[22]   In the case of lay [23] or non-exempt [24] institutes the reservation is to the ordinary of the place where the apostate resides, even temporarily.  It should be noted that though secular confessors can by common law absolve religious from all sins and censures reserved in the order, they cannot absolve from this censure because this is reserved by the Code itself, even though, in the case of exempt clerics, to superiors of the order,[25] nor can other bishops or ordinaries absolve these exempt clerics in virtue of Canon 2253, n. 3, for the canon says explicitly the reservation is to "their own major superiors," not their own ordinaries, and being a penal law must be strictly interpreted.[26]

Apostates, likewise, are *ipso facto* excluded from all "legitimate ecclesiastical acts" which means to exercise the office of administrator of ecclesiastical goods, to take any part whatsoever, except that of witness, in ecclesiastical trials, to act as *patrinus* in the sacraments

----

[15] Piat, *Praelectiones*, q. 216, 3, as to the observance of course the prescription of Canon 2232, § 1, holds good.

[16] Canon 2257, § 1.

[17] Canons 2259, § 1; 2260, 1240, § 1, n. 2; 2261, 2262, § 1; 2263, 2264, 2265, 1757, § 2, n. 1°; 1758.  *Cf.* Hyland, F. E., *Excommunication* (Washington, 1928), pp. 48ff.

[18] Canon 488, n. 8°.

[19] Canon 488, n. 4°.

[20] Canon 615.

[21] Canon 618, § 1.

[22] Canon 488, n. 2°.

[23] Canon 488, n. 4°.

[24] Canon 488, n. 2°.

[25] Ayrinhac, *Penal Legislation*, n. 359 a.

[26] Blat, *Commentarium*, "De Delictic et Poenis," V, n. 228.

of baptism or confirmation, to vote in ecclesiastical elections, and to exercise the right of patronage.[27]   He loses, moreover, all the privileges, both spiritual and temporal of his order, and this likewise by the very fact of apostasy.

None of these penalties is removed by the very fact of the apostate's return.  The excommunication must be absolved by the major superior or local ordinary as just explained, the vindictive punishments [28] dispensed, by the Holy See as regards privation of active and passive voice, by their own ordinary as regards the other penalties.[29]

Moreover, if they return, and it should be noted that they are bound to return and superiors to seek them and receive them back,[30] they forever lack active and passive voice, that is, can neither vote nor be voted for, and are to be punished by the superiors with the constitutional penalties for apostasy.

It should be also noted that all the penalties except this very last one, namely, the constitutional penalties, are *latae sententiae*.  Presumption is not required and hence crass or supine ignorance of either law or penalty will not excuse, and even invincible ignorance excuses only from the excommunication and not from the other penalties.[31]   The *ferendae sententiae* penalty is mandatory from the words *puniri debet*, "must be punished," and, therefore, subject to the prescriptions of Canon 2223, § 3, implicitly contained in this very canon.

After the decree of the Sacred Congregation of Religious of May 16, 1911, [32] apostasy from religion was punished with *ipso facto* dismissal, as it was also in the preliminary schemata of the Code.  Although it is not among those so punished by the Code it still seems to be sufficient cause for dismissal by the legitimate superior.[33]

---

[27] Canon 2256, n. 2; exception for trials in Canon 1654.

[28] Canon 2291, nn. 8, 9, 10, 11.

[29] Canon 2236, § 1.

[30] Canon 645.

[31] Canon 2229, § 3, n. 1°.

[32] *A. A. S.*, III (1911), 237, 238.

[33] Hippolytus a S. Familia, *Anal. O. C. D.* (1930), p. 162.

### ARTICLE 2.  FUGITIVES.  CANON 2386.

**Canon 2386.  Religiosus fugitivus ipso facto incurrit in privationem oficii, si quod in religione habeat, et in suspensionem proprio Superiori maiori reservatam, si sit in sacris; cum autem redierit, puniatur secundum constitutiones, et si constitutiones nihil de hoc caveant, Superiori maior pro gravitate culpae poenas infligat.***

The fugitive religious is defined as "one who, without the permission of his superiors, deserts the religious house but with the intention of returning." [84]  Evidently he differs in several respects from the apostate treated in the previous article, for in the first place any religious, that is, one who has made profession of vows in any institute,[85] and not only those who have made perpetual vows are included, but not, of course, postulants and novices, though the Pontifical Commission declared it applied even to members of clerical societies without vows.[86]  Even Cerato [87] and Cipollini [88] make no attempt to restrict its meaning to men.  Moreover, the fugitive only intends to withdraw temporarily from religious obedience and by no means to sever his connection with his institute.  This in fact constitutes the specific difference between the apostate and the fugitive.  However, it is the unanimous teaching of the authors that flight is not to be confounded with illicit exit from the house.  No norm is laid down in the common law for determining when a person is to

---

* Canon 2386.  The fugitive religious incurs *ipso facto* privation of office if he had one in his Institute, and, if he is in Sacred Orders, suspension reserved to his own higher superior; when he will have returned, he must be punished conformably to the constitutions, and if the constitutions make no provision for the case, the higher Superior shall inflict punishment according to the gravity of the fault.

[84] Canon 644, § 3.

[85] Canon 488, n. 7.

[86] *Pontificia Commissio ad Canones Codicis authentice Interpretanda*, 2, 3 June, 1918—*A. A. S.*, X (1918), 347.

[87] Cerato, *Censurae Vigentes*, p. 221.

[88] Cipollini, *De Censuris*, n. 116.

be adjudged a fugitive, but all concede that no matter how illicit the departure may have been he cannot be classed as a fugitive if he returns before nightfall. The norms may be laid down in the particular constitutions, as for example in the Order of Preachers one night's absence without permission begets the presumption that the man is a fugitive.[39] It may be safely said that unless particular laws determine otherwise a man should not be classed as a fugitive if his absence does not extend beyond two or three days.[40] Moreover, all admit that one who leaves his house, even without permission or against the local superior's prohibition, to go to his higher superior is not a fugitive though he loses exemption in virtue of Canon 616, § 1, should he enjoy it.

The penalty directed against clerics in major orders, namely, suspension, is a censure,[41] the other penalties vindictive. The suspension and privation of office are *latae sententiae,* the others *ferendae sententiae,* preceptive and indeterminate. Consequently, while crass and supine ignorance of either law or penalty will excuse from none of the penalties, invincible ignorance would excuse the cleric from suspension, but not the official from privation of office,[42] while the other penalties would have to be applied under the norms of the respective constitutions, or under the general principles of the Code which allow the mitigation, suspension and even cancellation of the penalties as explained above.[43] Before any penalty whatever is inflicted, however, the crime must be perfect and consummated [44] and an attempt, frustrated or abandoned, does not incur the penalties herein enumerated.

There remains one point to be discussed, hitherto not touched upon in this article, concerning the one to whom the suspension of

[39] *Constitutiones, Sacri Ordinis Praedictorum, Const.* 197, §§ II and V.

[40] Vermeersch-Creusen, *Epitome,* III, n. 590; Sole, o. c., 446; Ayrinhac, *Penal Legislation,* n. 360; Cipollini, n. 116.

[41] Since it is indefinite and not *"ad tempus praefinitum vel ad beneplacitum Superioris"* as is the vindictive penalty of suspension. Canon 2298, n. 2°. Vermeersch-Creusen, *Epitome,* III, n. 580; Cappello, *De Censuris,* n. 539; Cipollini, o. c., n. 116; Cerato, o. c., p. 221.

[42] Canon 2229, § 3, n. 1°.

[43] Canons 2223, § 3; 2288. Supra Chap. II, Art. 1.

[44] Canon 2242, § 1; Sole, o. c., 446; Cappello, o. c., n. 359.

clerics is reserved. The canon says "to the higher superiors" and unlike the preceding canon makes no provision for non-exempt clerical institutes. It may even happen as Creusen points out that in some institutes such as the Brothers of Charity of St. John of God, the superior may not even be a cleric.[45]

How, he asks, can one who has not jurisdiction or one incapable of obtaining jurisdiction, which can be obtained only by clerics [46] absolve in either forum from the censure? Chelodi [47] simply applies the rule of Canons 2385 and 2237 and states that the local ordinary has power to absolve. Creusen admits that in the case of institutes whose superiors are not clerics the local ordinary is their only major superior, which is not borne out by the Code,[48] and hence it is reserved to him. As for clerical non-exempt institutes he holds that the omission of the local ordinary is not unintentional and that though this is the only case in the Code where it is done the jurisdiction is herein delegated by law to the major superior of non-exempt clerics to absolve.[49]

The argument, though not without some merit, is weakened by the admission of the local ordinary in the case of lay superiors, and as Creusen himself says he would not be surprised to see the Pontifical Commission, by extensive interpretation apply the rule of Canon 2385. It does not, however, seem necessary to adopt such an explanation. One of the Hospitallers of St. John of God has risen to contradict the statement of Creusen and to demonstrate in a doctorate dissertation presented to the Athanaeum of St. Apollinaris that even the lay superiors of his order, and indeed of any exempt order, possess true jurisdiction.[50]

In the first place, the statement that the local ordinary is the

[45] Vermeersch-Creusen, *Epitome,* III, 590.

[46] Canon 118.

[47] Chelodi, *Jus Poenale,* n. 101, 2, p. 136, footnote 3.

[48] Canon 488, n. 8°, makes no distinction between clerical and lay institutes, and Canon 504 requires that major superiors be professed in the same institute.

[49] Vermeersch-Creusen, *Epitome,* III, 590.

[50] Saucedo, P. R., "*Exercitium Jurisdictionis et Superiores Laici ex Ordine Hospitalario S. Joannis de Deo,*" *Commentarium pro Religiosis,* XIII (1932), 51-61, 106-114, 224-231, 291-302.

major superior in that particular order at least is incorrect,[51] since the bishop has no more power over them than he has over any other regulars as he proves by the citation of many Papal documents, and the reservation of this canon is to their own major superior.[52]

Furthermore, he goes on to prove that laymen are incapable of jurisdiction only in virtue of Canon 118, that is, by ecclesiastical law, and that this general law may be and *de facto* is patently derogated by more special laws in the Code itself. In this he has the support of D'Annibale[53] and the patent case of Canon 219 as an example. Canon 239, § 2, admits that a layman can be, and in times past, has been elected Pope, and he obtains supreme jurisdiction from the moment of his acceptation, before consecration, ordination, tonsure even. Moreover, there have been many cases of delegation of jurisdiction to laymen in history, and there is no reason why the Holy See or the common law cannot do so today,[54] and in fact the Briefs and Bulls cited by the author establish beyond question the fact that in regard to this order, at least by privilege, such concession has been made.[55] Not content with this, however, he proceeds to prove that the nature of exemption requires jurisdiction within the order,[55a] for being withdrawn from the jurisdiction of local ordinaries these religious would otherwise be masterless men. Therefore, the special law of Canon 615 derogates from the general principle of Canon 118.

Accepting this thesis as proved, and the arguments seem quite irrefutable, Canon 2386 may be accepted strictly as it reads, and the higher superiors taken as higher superiors in the sense of Canon 488, n. 8°, more probably excepting the abbot primate and abbot praeses of monastic congregations in virtue of Canon 501, § 3.

[51] *Cf.* Canon 504, where it is required that superiors be professed religious of the same institute.

[52] Saucedo, p. 53.

[53] D'Annibale, J., *Summula Theologiae Moralis* (Rome, 1908), 5th ed., Vol. I, p. 59, "Ecclesiasticae jurisdictionis incapaces sunt, jure divino foeminae et non baptizati, canonico, laici."

[54] Saucedo, pp. 108, 109.

[55] *Ibid.*, pp. 226-231.

[55a] *Ibid.*, pp. 111-114, 302.

### ARTICLE 3.    FLIGHT WITH PERSON OF OPPOSITE SEX
### CANON 646, § 1, N. 2°

**Canon 646, § 1. Ipso facto habendi sunt tanquam legitime dimissi religiosi:**

**2°. Religiosus, qui fugam arripuerit cum muliere; aut religiosa quae cum viro.***

Having considered the crime of total abandonment of religion by apostasy, and temporary abandonment by flight, there remains only to be treated under this chapter on unlawful egress, the crime of elopement with one of the opposite sex.

The canon applies in the first place to all religious without distinction, no matter to what institute or class of institutes they belong, whether they be perpetually or temporarily professed, and even to members of societies living in common without vows.[56]  The very fact of committing the crime—in this case eloping with one of the opposite sex—brings with it automatically the penalty of dismissal, and the declaration prescribed in § 2 of this same canon is not necessary for the effectiveness of the penalty.[57]  The disappearance or flight, however, must be public, not only external and public by nature, but publicly known and provable in court in the sense of Canons 1037 and 2197, n. 3.[58]  Thus, if any element, either that of flight, or that of being with person of opposite sex was occult, the dismissal does not take effect.[59]  However, mere flight in the sense of Canon 644, § 3, with the intention of returning is sufficient to bring on this penalty, provided there be found complicity with one of the

---

*Canon 646, § 1. The following religious are *ipso facto* regarded as lawfully dismissed.

2°.  A religious who will have run away with a person of the opposite sex. (Authorised English Translation.)

[56] Canon 681.  *Cf.* Supra Chap. I, in princ.

[57] Pont. Com., July 30, 1934—*A. A. S.*, XXVI (1934), 494, which applies also to Chap. I and Chap. X, Art. 3.

[58] Schäfer, *De Religiosis*, n. 576; Leitner, *Handbuch*, p. 462.

[59] S. Goyenche, "*Consultationes*," n. 20, in *Commetarium Pro Religiosis*, IX (1928), pp. 428, 429.

opposite sex, nor does it matter in the least how long they may be together. The penalty is incurred by "taking flight." [60]

Granting the flight to have been public and with a person of the opposite sex, does the dismissal necessarily follow in all cases? That is, does the accompaniment by any person of the opposite sex suffice, even though only material, as for instance the taxicab driver who drives and therefore materially accompanies a fugitive sister to the train? Blat,[61] Fanfani,[62] Bastien [63] and Palombo [64] all respond in the affirmative, admitting no distinction and holding all women, even those below the age of puberty as included under this canon. Schäfer,[65] Leitner,[66] Wernz-Vidal,[67] Hippolytus a S. Familia,[68] Chelodi,[69] Tabera [70] and Vermeersch [71] all respond negatively, requiring formal complicity, or qualified flight. Tabera, Hippolytus and Vermeersch require also a libidinous intention. The argument for the affirmative is based solely on a strict and even literal interpretation of the law, while the argument for the negative, based more on the reason of the law and fitness of things interprets it through its source, and the argument is best set forth by the Carmelite writer who, referring back to the decree of the Sacred Congregation of Religious [72] from which this canon is taken deduces from the close connection between this qualified flight and attempted mar-

[60] Schäfer, *l. c.;* Leitner, *l. c.;* Goyenche, *l. c.;* Coronata, pp. 845, 846b; Wernz-Vidal *Jus Canonicum,* n. 438; Fanfani, *De Jure Rel.,* n. 496, 20; Tabera, A., *De Dimissione Religiosorum,* in *Commentarium Pro Religiosis,* Vol. XI (1930), pp. 415-418.

[61] Blat, *Comment., "De Personis,"* II, n. 726.

[62] Fanfani, o. c., n. 496, 20.

[63] Bastien, *Directoire Canonique,* n. 209 and note 4.

[64] Palombo, *De Dimiss. Rel.,* p. 236, footnote 3.

[65] Schäfer, *l. c.*

[66] Leitner, *l. c.*

[67] Wernz-Vidal, *l. c.*

[68] Hippolytus a S. Familia in *Analecta Ordinis Carmelitarum Discalceatorum,* Vol. IV (1929), pp. 160, 161.

[69] Chelodi, *Jus de Personis* (Trent, 1927), n. 289a, note 2.

[70] Tabera, *l. c.*

[71] Vermeersch, *"De Fuga cum Persona Alterius sexus in casu,"* Canon 646, § 1, n. 2, in *Periodica,* XIX (1923), 121*.

[72] S. C. de Rel., 16 May, 1911—*A. A. S.,* III (1911), 238.

riage that a libidinous end is required.  As he says, otherwise nothing more notably criminal would be had except simple flight.  Hence, he concludes flight with a near relative, at least in direct line or first degree collateral, or with a child below the age of puberty, would not incur the penalty.

Tabera, however, does not go so far.  He demands qualified flight, which is the coalescence of material or formal complicity of a person of opposite sex, and that the flight be taken with lustful intent.  He grants that flight with relatives in direct line or first degree collateral is not qualified, but denies that flight with one below the age of puberty is not.  He says rightly that there may be material, as in the case of rape, or even formal complicity in the lustful object on the part of one below puberty, and that a religious fleeing with the child for that purpose is dismissed.  Thus, also, Wernz-Vidal and Palombo.  Both Tabera and Hippolytus agree that even in cases of adults, but more especially so in those of children, the fugitive may prove the absence of libidinous intent and thereby escape dismissal, the burden of proof of course being on him.  While the solution of Tabera seems comformable to law and reason, it might be modified somewhat regarding the proof of absence of libidinous intent.  It would seem better to say that dismissal might be escaped should the flight, even in its external circumstances, lack the character of being "with a person of the opposite sex;" that is, from the nature of the case as externally manifested no lustful intention could be presumed to have been in the background.

All admit that the accompaniment need not be material, that simple flight with an agreement to meet and go together incurs the penalty; that concubinage immediately following flight, if the parties knew each other before, would raise the presumption against them; that simple concubinage or even concubinage during apostasy does not come under this cannon; that fugitive egress, even for the sake of sinning by lust, and even though frequently repeated, does not fall under this law.  Further, one who goes out with permission and then makes a journey with a woman or women is not a fugitive and hence not dismissed, unless by so doing he withdraws himself from religious obedience.

The penalty is *latae sententiae*, does not require presumption, and is not a censure. Hence, neither ignorance of the law nor of the penalty excuses.[73] As soon as the fact of flight with one of the other sex is known publicly, and the lustful end known or justly presumed, the guilty party is dismissed from religion, nor is he to be sought after and received back under Canon 672. *Ipso facto* dismissal is final.[74]

[73] Canon 2229, § 3, n. 1.

[74] *Pont. Com.*, July 30, 1934—A. A. S., XXVI (1934), 494.

# CHAPTER IX

## PROFESSION INVALIDATED BY FRAUD

### Canon 2387

**Canon 2387. Religiosus clericus cuius professio ob admissum ab ipso dolum nulla fuerit declarata, si sit in minoribus ordinibus constitutus, e statu clericali abiiciatur; si in maioribus, ipso facto suspensus manet, donec Sedi Apostolicae aliter visum fuerit.***

The penalty contained in this canon for nullifying through fraud one's own profession applies only to those religious who are clerics. For others, the invalidity of the act is considered penalty enough, but in the case of clerics an additional element enters in. Every cleric must be ascribed to a certain diocese or a certain religious institute. Those presented for ordination by the superiors of a religious institute are ordained for the service of that institute and ascribed to it, not to the diocese.[1] Now the canonical bond existing between him and his institute, on which its claim to his service is based, rests on his profession. If this proves null, the claim is baseless and he is practically a vagrant cleric, a condition condemned by Canon 111. Were this brought about through his own fault, that is, his own fraud, it merits severe punishment.[2]

From the nature of the law it is evident that only those who have received clerical tonsure come under it, but all religious who have this tonsure are included, whether they have solemn or simple, temporary or perpetual vows, or belong to pontifical or diocesan insti-

---

* Canon 2387. A religious cleric whose profession shall have been declared null on account of fraud committed by himself is to be dismissed from the clerical state if he be in minor orders; if in majors he remains suspended until the Holy See shall provide otherwise.

[1] Canon 111.

[2] Ayrinhac, *Penal Legislation*, n. 361; Chelodi, *Jus Poenale*, n. 101, 3.

tutes, and even members of societies without vows who live in community under a superior.[3]

The profession here referred to may be either simple or solemn, temporary or perpetual, or in the societies without vows, the equivalent agreement which takes the place of profession. The law makes no distinction.[4]

However, the mere fact of nullity of profession, even though it be through fraud, that is, deceit in falsely alleging or concealing something which if known would have prevented the profession,[5] does not carry with it this penalty. The fraud must have been committed by the one making the profession, not by some one else unknown to him, and Cappello [6] states that even if he consents to this fraud on the part of some one else he does not incur the penalty. This can only be admitted when the consent does not implicate the person himself in the fraud. The further assertion that a cleric through whose fault some one else is fraudulently professed does not incur [7] is evident, as it is not the offense under consideration.

The fraud and consequent invalidity of profession must of course be certain, and proved, and the declaration of nullity therefrom must be given. Pending sentence, no matter how certain the fraud, the penalties do not become operative.[8]

What if the admission to the novitiate were invalid because of fraud committed by the candidate?[9] The response would seem to be under a distinction. If the impediment concealed by fraud is kept secret throughout the entire novitiate, and especially at the end because it is a cause for dismissal, the profession itself would seem null because of fraud. If, however, the impediment were known or dispensed during the novitiate, the profession would be declared null

---

[3] *Pont. Com.*, 2, 3 June, 1918—A. A. S., IX (1918), 347.

[4] Sole, o. c., n. 447; Blat, *Commentarium,* "*De Delictis et Poenis,*" V, n. 230; Ayrinhac, *Penal Legislation*, n. 361.

[5] Canon 572, § 1, n. 4°.

[6] Cappello, *De Censuris,* n. 528.

[7] *Ibid., l. c.*

[8] *Ibid.,* n. 529.

[9] Canon 542, n. 1.

not because of fraud, but because of the nullity of the novitiate. It must be seen on what ground the profession was declared null.[10]

If the cleric be in minor orders he is to be dismissed from the clerical state, that is, laicized by decree of the local ordinary.[11] If he be in major orders—subdeacon or above—he remains suspended until the Holy See sees fit to dispense him. The dismissal is *ferendae sententiae*, but the suspension is *latae sententiae* as is evident from the term *"manet,"* though it is a vindictive penalty. This is clear from the fact that it lasts not until the guilty one recedes from his contumacy, but until the Holy See, or one specially delegated by the Holy See, decides otherwise.[12] Ignorance does not excuse from either of these penalties.[18]

[10] Cappello, o. c., n. 528; Vermeersch-Creusen, *Epitome*, III, n. 591.
[11] Canon 211, § 2.
[12] Canon 2248, § 3.
[18] Canon 2229, § 3, n. 1.

# CHAPTER X

## SACRILEGIOUS MARRIAGE

Article 1. Attempted by Solemnly Professed Regulars
Canon 2388, § 1

**Canon 2388, § 1. . . . Regulares aut moniales post votum sollemne castitatis . . . matrimonium etiam civiliter tantum contrahere praesumentes, incurrunt in excommunicationem latae sententiae Sedi Apostolicae simpliciter reservatam.***

The earliest and most numerous penal laws enacted against religious were for offenses against the vow of chastity. The earliest Council whose acts have come down to us [1] enacts a most severe penalty against those unfaithful to this vow, and subsequent legislation of the early Church is filled with such laws. Today the only penalty in the common law of the Church against religious as such who violate this vow is the one in this present canon, and it only affects those who marry or attempt to marry.

The present article treats only of those named in the first paragraph of this canon, namely, those who have actually taken solemn vows; not regulars under simple vows,[2] nor nuns whose vows are simple by prescription of the Holy See,[3] nor *a fortiori*, novices or postulants in religious orders.

---

* Canon 2388, § 1. . . . Regulars or nuns after the solemn vow of chastity . . . presuming to contract even only civil marriage, incur excommunication *latae sententiae* reserved *simpliciter* to the Holy See.

[1] Council of Elvira, c. 305, A. D. Canon 13, incorporated into Gratian's Decree, C. 25, CXXVII, q. 1. *Cf.* note 38, Chap. I, Part I, supra. Two other early Councils, Neocaesarea (325) and Ancyra (314) enacted similar legislation, but as these were only particular councils and their laws were not incorporated in Gratian's Decree, they were omitted in the historical part of this work.

[2] Canon 574 regarding temporary profession of simple vows for three years before solemn profession.

[3] Canon 488, n. 7.

The crime punished is "presuming to contract marriage, even only civilly." Because of the diriment impediment of, at least, solemn vows [4] and in the case of civil marriage because of defect of form [5] likewise these solemnly professed religious cannot truly and validly contract marriage; they can only "attempt" it, that is, observe some formality manifesting the intention of forming a marriage contract and intending as far as in their power lies, to form such a contract; one recognized at least by civil law, or *a fortiori*, by a false religion.[6] Concubinage does not come under this law unless it be such as is recognized in some places as "common law marriage" in which case, when the requirements are fulfilled, it becomes a civil marriage in those places and hence falls under this canon.[7]

So also does any form of marriage or appearance of marriage entered into even though besides the impediment of solemn vows, there were other impediments such as consanguinity, affinity, or the like.[8] If, however, the contract be null for want of consent, that is, because the consent was merely simulated and not really given at all, the general opinion, opposed by Cerato,[9] is that the censure would not be incurred.[10]

The arguments of Cerato are: 1°, that marriage in itself valid is not required for contracting the censure; 2°, that "internal consent of the mind is always presumed conformed to the words or signs shown in celebrating marriage [11] and, therefore, the censure is to be pre-

[4] Canon 1073.

[5] Canon 1094.

[6] Ayrinhac, *Penal Legislation*, n. 362; Sole, n. 488, 3°; Blat, *Commentarium*, "De Delictis et Poeins," V, n. 231.

[7] Cocchi, G., *Commentarium in Codicem Juris Canonici* (Taurinae-Augustae, 1931), Book II, Part II, n. 145c; Fanfani, *De Jure Reg.*, n. 496, 3°; Schäfer, *De Religiosis*, n. 576.

[8] S. C. S. Off., 13 January, 1892—*Act Sanctae Sedis*, XXIV (1892), 625, 626.

[9] Cerato, *Censurae Vigentes*, pp. 131, 132.

[10] Sole, o. c., n. 488, 3; Ayrinhac, *Penal Legislation*, n. 362; Vermeersch-Creusen, *Epitome*, III, n. 592, 2; Cappello, *De Censuris*, n. 355; Cipollini, *De Censuris*, n. 61, p. 158; Hippolytus a S. Familia, pp. 160-162; Tabera, "De Dimmis Rel.," *Com. pro. Rel.*, XI (1930), 415-418; Pistocchi, M., I, *Canoni Penali* (Taurino, 1925), p. 317, et alii.

[11] Canon 1086, § 1.

sumed in the external forum until the simulation is proved.  3. In a crime which of its very nature requires an accomplice both parties are culpable in the same way unless it appears otherwise from the things connected with it,[12] and in this case it does not appear otherwise.[13]

Sole, adhering to the opinion of pre-Code authors, sums up the case in this way: "Who feigns to place an act, seems to place the act, but really does not place it, and the force of simulation is this, that if the value of the act placed, *e. g.*, matrimony, depended only on his own will he would not contract valid matrimony.  Because, therefore, the censure falls on those who *presume, dare, attempt*, to enter matrimony and the ones feigning to contract are not such, we think they escape the censure."[14]  Thus, also, Creusen: "Who feigns consent does not attempt the marriage contract."[15]  So, too, Tabera: "When one fictitiously and feignedly consents the element which constitutes an attempt should rather be said to be lacking, and hence attempted matrimony is not had."[16]  Hippolytus a S. Familia in treating of Canon 646, § 1, n. 3, says: "What of him who feigns to contract?  He does not incur, because in order that one be said to attempt a crime it is required that he seriously, knowingly and willingly places the act ordained to the execution of it, and when it is required that the attempt be brought to an act of itself sufficient to perform the crime, then, if the attempt does not produce its effect that ought to depend on another cause outside the will of the agent.  And so, in order that one attempt marriage it is necessary that he place the necessary act with the true intention of contracting as far as possible, and if it is null, that depends on some cause outside his own mind."[17]

Cerato responds that "who simulates consent does not simulate the act of matrimony which he celebrates with the entire form of celebration, nor does it seem to make any difference that the force of

---

[12] Canon 2209, § 2.

[13] Cerato, *l. c.*

[14] Sole, o. c., n. 488, 3.

[15] Vermeersch-Creusen, *Epitome*, III, n. 592, 2.

[16] Tabera, *l. c.*

[17] Hippolytus a S. Familia, *Anal. O. C. D.*, IV (1930), 160-162.

simulation invalidates the act, because the validity of the marriage does not matter. Nor has the exception based on the word "presume" any value for unless we wish arbitrarily to derogate the prescription of Canon 2229, § 2, the word "presume" is to be taken as meaning full knowledge of law and fact and full deliberation about the crime.[18]

The response to Cerato's three arguments is given by Sole and others: His first argument has nothing to do with the case. True, valid marriage is not required but it is not the act but the fact (daring or presumption) that the law coerces, for that the fact may be called true it is necessary that nothing of its nature essential be lacking to it, that is, that at another time it may exist at least by natural law. Nor does the second argument prove anything, because from the fact that the consent is presumed it merely follows that the simulation would have to be proved,[19] and hence the censure is always presumed, not always incurred.[20] As to the third point, as Creusen says, he is postulating what is to be proved. "Who simulates consent certainly is an accomplice in the offense if the other offends, but where only one consents the contract is deficient of itself as in the case of substantial error or fear, hence neither the one consenting nor the one feigning consent offends."[21] As for Cerato's rebuttal, his first point is basically the same as his first principal argument, and the same response may be given, namely, that a real marriage is not required but a real intention to commit the crime punished with the censure is required, and this intention is lacking when one voluntarily omits something which is of its nature essential, namely, consent. Nor is his second point of rebuttal convincing, for granted that "presume" according to Canon 2229, § 2, requires full knowledge of law and fact together with full deliberation, it also requires that the act known and deliberated upon follow, that is, the will to contract marriage, effective as far as the agent himself can

----

[18] Cerato, o. c., nn. 131, 132.

[19] Sole, o. c., 488, 3.

[20] Vermeersch-Creusen, *Epitome*, n. 592, 2; Hippolytus a S. Familia, *l. c.;* Tabera, *l. c.*

[21] Vermeersch-Creusen, *Epitome, l. c.*

make it so. Certainly such is not the case when one after full deliberation does not will to contract but merely to feign marriage.

It is quite true that many strange anomalies may arise as a consequence of this interpretation. Postulating Creusen's argument cited just above that deficiency of consent of either party exempts from the penalty one might find the case, for instance, where a nun deliberately wills to and in fact does enter into a civil marriage with a man who merely simulates consent. She, with full knowledge of law and penalty, and full malicious intent, would be excused from the censure because of the simulation on the part of the man, since "where only one consents the contract is *per se* deficient," and, therefore, the crime of contracting marriage was not committed. This hardly seems reasonable, yet the same conclusion would be reached were grave fear or substantial error, rather than simulation, the cause of lack of consent. For example, a monk may force a girl, through grave fear, to go through a marriage ceremony with him, and yet escape the censure because her consent was vitiated, the contract was *per se* deficient, and the crime of contracting marriage not committed. It seems, therefore, as though Creusen's rebuttal of Cerato's third argument falls through the *reductio ad absurdum*, and since it proves too much, proves nothing.

Must then Cerato's argument be conceded in spite of the opinion of so many illustrious doctors, and must it be concluded that although by the simulation of consent the regular or nun may escape the censure directly, they nevertheless incur indirectly as necessary accomplices in virtue of Canons 2209, § 2, and 2231?

Considering the jurisprudence now in effect concerning penal laws, the strict interpretation to be given them,[22] the more benign interpretation they are to receive and the prohibition to extend them from case to case or from person to person even when an equal or stronger reason exists,[23] and the restriction always to be placed on odious things,[24] the negative answer seems to be the more probable. The arguments of Sole are sound and the fact that the argument of Creusen can be used to allow greater criminals to evade punishment

[22] Canon 19.
[23] Canon 2219, §§ 1 and 3.
[24] Reg. 15, R. J., in VI°.

does not nullify it in law. It is necessary to accept and stand by the probable consequences.

Nor does recourse to Canon 132, § 2, solve the problem. This canon declares clerics in minor orders *ipso jure* dismissed from the clerical state if they marry, unless the marriage was null from fear or force suffered by them. The case is similar to the one in hand but it is here a question of penalties and Canon 20 expressly forbids the application of penalties according to the norms of laws dealing with similar cases.

The most reasonable solution would seem to be that the party placing the act with full malice and presumption should incur regardless of the dispositions of the other party, but it does not seem to have support in the law as it stands. Most likely the Commission, if asked, would respond that the guilty party incurred, but it has not yet so declared and until it does Creusen's argument, with its consequences, must prevail.

All agree that the censure is not incurred by one who contracts through error or grave fear, though as Cerato [25] rightly says it is because of the presumption required [26] and not because of the essential invalidity of the marriage. Some [27] allege even light fear as an excusing cause, but this is not borne out in the law, unless the fear be at least relatively grave [28] and is in fact rejected by other authors.[29]

As has already been seen presumption in the commission of this offense is required before the penalty is incurred. This means, according to Canon 2229, § 2, that lack of full knowledge or deliberation or in fact anything which in any way diminishes the imputability of the act either on the part of the intellect or on the part of the will, excuses from the penalty.

The penalty is excommunication, contracted by the very fact of entering into the attempted marriage, and reserved simply to the Holy See. Consequently one can only be absolved from this censure by the Sacred Penitentiary or some one having faculties to absolve

---

[25] Cerato, *Censurae Vigentes*, pp. 131, 132.

[26] Canon 2229, § 2.

[27] Cappello, *De Censuris*, n. 356, 3; Ayrinhac, *Penal Legislation*, n. 362.

[28] Canon 2205, § 2.

[29] Sole, o. c., 488, 3, footnote 3; Cerato, o. c., pp. 131, 132.

from such censures, in the internal forum. In the external forum application should be made to the Sacred Congregation of Religious.

As is evident, before the contumacy may be said to have ceased the parties must either have separated, or the one bound by solemn vows have had them dispensed and a true marriage contracted.

ARTICLE 2. ATTEMPTED OR CONTRACTED BY RELIGIOUS WITH SIMPLE PERPETUAL VOWS. CANON 2388, § 2

**Canon 2388, § 2. Quod si [religiosi praesumentes matrimonium etiam civiliter tantum contrahere] sint professi votorum simplicium perpetuorum tam in Ordinibus quam in Congregationibus religiosis, omnes, ut supra, excommunicatio tenet latae sententiae Ordinario reservata.***

Those affected by this part of the canon are all perpetually professed religious who were not included under the first paragraph, that is, all whose vows are simple but perpetual, whether these be members of an order, such as Jesuit scholastics and nuns whose vows are simple by apostolic prescription, or of a congregation, whether pontifical or diocesan. Those whose vows are only temporary are not included here, nor do they contract any censure by marrying in virtue of either paragraph of this canon. There is some dispute, now little more than academic, as to whether those who previous to the Code took simple perpetual vows for three years before solemn profession are included. Blat [30] affirms, Cappello [31] denies. These vows were perpetual on the part of the religious, but not on the part of the institute. Hence, Cappello concludes they were not absolutely perpetual, and so further concludes they are not included here. The reason alleged is not convincing, bearing in mind the strict interpretation to be given penal laws. This canon speaks of simple per-

---

* Canon 2388, § 2. But if they [religious who marry or attempt marriage, even merely civil marriage] be professed of simple perpetual vows as well in Orders as in religious congregations, all, as above, incur excommunication *latae sententiae* reserved to the Ordinary.

[30] Blat, *Commentarium*, "De Delictis et Poenis," V, n. 231.
[31] Cappello, *De Censuris*, n. 395, 3.

petual vows; those vows were simple and perpetual, perpetual *simpliciter* if not absolutely. Moreover, they were perpetual on the part of the religious and it would be the religious, not the institute, who would be violating them by marrying. Today the only practical application of this question would come in the case of a person who has been out of the Church for several years and is seeking reconciliation.

Persons with simple vows can ordinarily contract a valid marriage, unless by apostolic privilege a nullifying effect on marriage has been attached to them, as in the case of the Jesuits, or another and diriment impediment stands in the way. For the incurring of the excommunication now under consideration it makes no difference whether or not the marriage is valid, and everything said on that score in the preceding article is equally applicable here, even as to the case of simulation of consent and fear or error. So, too, do those things hold here which were there laid down regarding the imputability required because of the use of the word "presume."

In this case, however, the excommunication, contracted by the very fact of the marriage, is reserved only to the ordinary. According to some [32] this means the local ordinary for lay or non-exempt religious and the major superiors, provincials and the like for exempt clerics. Pruemmer [33] says, "The ordinary seems to be he to whom the persons sinning are actually subject." Admitting both these solutions to be true they seem only partial and the one given by Blat [34] and Cerato [35] seems to be that of the Code itself, for no distinction is made and hence any ordinary in whose territory they happen to be even temporarily, or as *peregrini,* or their own proper ordinary, whether bishop or provincial, can absolve.[36] Recession from contumacy in this case would require a dispensation from the vows, or, if the marriage were invalid, either separation of the parties or a convalidation of the marriage.

[32] Cappello, *De Censuris,* n. 396, n. 2; Vermeersch-Creusen, *Epitome,* III, 592, 2; Ayrinhac, *Penal Legislation,* n. 362.

[33] Pruemmer, *Manuale J. C.,* q. 226.

[34] Blat, *Commentarium,* V, n. 231.

[35] Cerato, *Censure Vigentes,* p. 105.

[36] Canon 2253, 3°.

### ARTICLE 3. MARRIAGE ATTEMPTED OR CONTRACTED BY ANY RELIGIOUS. CANON 646, § 1, N. 3°

#### 1. *Ipso Jure Dismissal*

**Canon 646, § 1. Ipso facto habendi sunt tanquam legitime dimissi religiosi:**
**3°. Attentantes aut contrahentes matrimonium aut etiam vinculum, ut aiunt, civile.***

This canon is much wider in extent than either or both parts of Canon 2388, which affects only religious of perpetual vows. This canon refers to all religious of solemn and simple, perpetual and temporary vows, of pontifical and diocesan institutes and even to societies living in common without vows,[37] though not to novices or postulants.

The offense, too, is more comprehensive than in the other canon, for though all who incur the excommunication there prescribed incur likewise *ipso facto* dismissal, dismissal may be incurred even when the excommunication is not. All that was true there regarding the indifference as to validity or invalidity of the marriage is likewise true here, as is also the fact that concubinage without the semblance of at least civil or common law marriage is not included.[38] So, too, are the conclusions regarding simulated consent or lack of consent through grave fear or error,[39] though these conclusions are not in

---

* Canon 646, § 1, n. 3. The following religious are *ipso facto* regarded as lawfully dismissed:
3°. Religious who attempt or contract marriage, even the so-called civil marriage. (Authorised English Translation.)

[37] Canon 681.

[38] Schäfer, *De Religiosis*, n. 576; Hippolytus a S. Familia, "De Dimiss Rel.," *Anal. O. C. D.*, IV (1930), pp. 160, 161; Tabera, *Di Dimiss Rel.—Com. pro Rel.*, XI (1930), pp. 915-918; Coronata, *Institutiones*, p. 846; Bastien, *Directoire Canonique*, p. 129, note 1; Cocchi, *Commentarium*, II, II, n. 145c; Fanfani, *De Jure Rel.*, 496, 3.

[39] Leitner, *Handbuch*, p. 462; Schäfer, o. c., n. 576; Coronata, o. c., p. 486; Chelodi, *Jus de Personis*, n. 289; Palombo, *De Dimiss Rel.*, n. 197, 3, note 3; Hippolytus a S. Familia, *l. c.*; Tabera, *l. c.*

this case based on the daring required by the use of the word presume [40] which is not found in this canon, but rather on the nature of
"attempt" as explained by Hippolytus and Tabera [41] in regard to
simulation, and on the principles regarding error [42] and grave fear[43]
laid down in the Code.   In regard to the simulation of consent, however, it must be noted here, and it applies to all three sections of this
chapter, that the fact of simulation must be proven, and that until
it is, the penalties, both excommunication and dismissal are always
presumed though not always incurred.

Likewise, it should be recognized in regard to both these canons
that the penalties are contracted even by apostates from religion or
dismissed religious who have not yet been released from their vows,
though here, too, simple concubinage following apostasy or dismissal
does not bring either the excommunication or the *ipso facto* dismissal
and the special effects which follow it, namely, ineligibility to return.[44]

For the rest it may be said that though this penalty is *latae sententiae* it is not a censure but a vindictive penalty, and presumption is not required for incurring it.   Hence, no sort of ignorance excuses from the penalty.[45]


### 2.   *Irregularity.   Canon 985, n. 3°*

Canon 985.   Sunt irregulares ex delicto:
3°.   Qui matrimonium attentare aut civilem tantum
actum ponere ausi sunt, vel ipsemet . . . votis religiosis
etiam simplicibus ac temporariis ligati, vel cum muliere
iisdem votis adstricta . . . *

---

[40] Canon 2229, § 2.
[41] Supra Art. I of this chapter.
[42] Canon 2202, §§ 1 and 3.
[43] Canon 2205, § 2.
[44] Pont. Com., 30 July, 1934—*A. A. S.*, XXVI (1934), p. 494.
[45] Canon 2229, § 3, n. 1°.
* Canon 985.   They are irregular from crime:
3°.   Who have dared to attempt marriage . . . either themselves being
bound by religious vows, even simple and temporary, or with a woman bound
by the same vows. . . .

In addition to the excommunication incurred by religious of perpetual vows, and *ipso jure* dismissal incurred by all religious who marry or attempt to marry, even only civilly,[46] they also incur irregularity.

Irregularity may be defined as an impediment which of itself, perpetually prohibits reception and exercise of orders. The reception of the orders, and indeed of every clerical grade including first tonsure [47] is primarily prohibited, and the exercise of the orders secondarily and as a consequence.[48]  It is not a penalty, properly so called, but rather an obstacle to the accession to or exercise of clerical orders, placed rather with a view to maintaining the dignity of the state and orders than to punishing or correcting the individual. However, the irregularities arising from crime partake very much of the nature of penalties and are considered after the manner of penalties, hence might properly be considered in a treatise on penal law.

The irregularity in this case is contracted by anyone bound by religious vows, even though only simple and temporary, who either contracts a valid marriage, or attempts to contract when he cannot validly do so, or even merely goes through the civil form of marriage.  As was said above regarding the penalties for this offense, it makes no difference whether or not the marriage is invalid from some other cause, as for instance consanguinity, or indeed it may be perfectly valid, though of course illicit. The irregularity, like all irregularities, is incurred by the very fact of marrying or attempting marriage.  Ignorance of the irregularity does not excuse from it,[49] but since the canon uses the term *ausi sunt* anything which lessens the imputability whether on the part of the intellect or on the part

---

[46] Canons 2388 and 646, § 1, n. 2, respectively.

[47] Canon 950.

[48] Pruemmer, *Manuale Juris Canonici*, q. 321; Vermeersch-Creusen, *Epitome*, II, n. 252; Blat, *Commentarium*, etc., "*De Sacramentis*," III, Part I, n. 337; Hickey, J. J., *Irregularities and Simple Impediments, in the New Code of Canon Law* (Washington, 1920), 9ff.

[49] Canon 988.

of the will, might seem to excuse.[50]   However it must be borne in mind that the irregularity is not properly speaking a penalty, but rather a safeguard of the clerical dignity, so the solution of the question of ignorance in this regard must be made with reservations.   If the ignorance is such as to excuse from mortal sin, then it excuses indirectly from the irregularity.   Otherwise it would seem it does not; for from Canon 988 ignorance of the irregularity does not excuse, and neither does ignorance of the law, which is a disabling law from which ignorance does not excuse [51] unless it is expressly so stated.

As has been said, the law affects all religious, but from the nature of the case it applies only to men, as women are ineligible for orders by nature.   However, it applies to women in a sense inasmuch as they can infect their accomplices with irregularity when they, being bound by religious vows, marry or attempt marriage.

It should be noted that the vows mentioned in the canon are *religious vows*, that is public vows made in a religious institute, with particular reference to the vow of chastity.   Therefore, members of societies without vows are not included, nor are those who have taken purely private vows of virginity, perfect chastity and the like, whether in societies or as individuals.   As regards those who were professed in a religious institute and afterwards dispensed from their vows of poverty and obedience, the original vow of chastity remaining intact, Creusen would excuse them from the irregularity, on the ground that the vow is no longer a religious vow.[52]   This reasoning does not seem correct.   The vow was certainly taken as a religious vow; the dispensation of the other vows did not reduce this from a public to a private vow, nor in fact alter its character in any way; it was left as it was, therefore as a religious vow.   However, one bound by such a vow is not irregular for marrying in violation of it, because this canon uses the plural form "bound by religious vows," and the party in question is bound not by *vows*, but merely by *a vow*.

The irregularity may be dispensed by the Sacred Congregation of Religious in the external forum and the Sacred Penitentiary in

---

[50] Canon 2229, § 2.

[51] Canon 16, *cf.* also Hickey, *Irregularities*, etc., pp. 84, 85.

[52] Vermeersch-Creusen, *Epitome*, II, n. 257, 3°.

the internal forum; or if the case is occult, which would be difficult though possible in this instance, the ordinary, local for non-exempt, major superior for clerical exempt institutes, may dispense.[53]   It might be remarked that at the present time a dispensation from this irregularity is very rarely if ever granted.

[53] Canon 990, § 1.

# CHAPTER XI

## Violation of the Common Life [1]

### Canon 2389

Canon 2389. Religiosi legem vitae communis constitutionibus prescriptae in re notabili violantes, graviter moneantur et, emendatione non secuta, puniantur etiam privatione vocis activae et passivae et, si Superiores sint, etiam officii.[*]

ALTHOUGH common life is not essential to religious life considered in the abstract [2] under the present discipline it is an essential element in the concrete and imposed on all religious institutes.[3]  It is defined, or rather described by Schäfer as follows: "Common life or community of goods consists in this, that by force of incorporation of each of the religious in the community all the temporal goods and income be administered in common.  Each religious should receive from these goods those things necessary for the sustenance of life and clothing according to the Constitutions."[4]  The Code

---

[1] This canon dealing with the penalty for violation of the Common Life was exhaustively treated by Rev. S. J. Turner, C.P., in his dissertation on the *Vow of Poverty* submitted to the Faculty of Canon Law of the Catholic University of America in 1929 for the degree of Doctor of Both Laws.  This work being the latest and most thorough on the subject the present chapter will be for the most part based on it, though it covers more territory than falls within the scope of this chapter.

[*] Canon 2389.  Religious who violate in a notable matter the law of common life prescribed by the Constitutions, must be seriously admonished and, if no amendment follows, punished even by the privation of active and passive voice and, if superiors, of office also.  (Authorised English Translation.)

[2] St. Thomas Aquinas, IIa-IIae, q. 188, Art. 8.

[3] Canons 487, 594.

[4] Schäfer, *De Religiosis*, n. 337. Although common life in its broad sense takes in much more than community of goods, as for instance common recreation, spiritual exercises in common, etc., it has come to be accepted in its narrowest sense

prescribes that this common life be carefully observed by all,[5] and in this canon punishes the violation of it.

As has been seen in the historical development of this subject the crimes against religious poverty and the common life have been punished in the past with many and severe penalties. Nevertheless, the law of Canon 2389 is new with the Code, inasmuch as both the offense punished and the punishment differ from what was laid down in the former law. The Tridentine decree [6] which punished violators with privation of active and passive voice for two years and other penalties according to their own constitutions, was generally interpreted as applying only to those who unlawfully retained money or property; not to those who spent the money or gave away the property.[7] The present law applies to all who violate the common life prescribed by the respective constitutions in any way. It applies to all religious without exception and even to members of societies without vows where the common life is observed.[8]

The sanction of this canon extends to whatever the constitutions prescribe relative to the common life,[9] but only violations of the common life as laid down in the respective constitutions are liable to the punishment. Thus the norm is purely relative, within certain limits. Prescriptions of constitutions contrary to the Code cannot be a true norm, unless these constitutions have received Papal approbation since the Code with express exemption. On the other hand immemorial customs against the constitutions or the Code itself, if they are tolerated,[10] serve as a true norm, and needless to say indults of exemption held by individual religious are in no way affected.

---

as meaning common purse and community of goods. Naturally in applying it to penal law it must be accepted in its strictest sense and extended no farther than necessary. *Cf.* Wernz-Vidal, *Jus Canonicum*, III, *"De Religiosis,"* p. 379, n. 371. Since it is largely from the violation of common life regarding goods and money that other violations flow it was perhaps deemed sufficient to punish this type of violation to halt the others.

[5] Canon 594.

[6] Conc. Trid., Sess. XXV, *de regularibus*, cap. 2.

[7] Piat, *Praelectiones J. R.*, I, q. 286, B. 2; Turner, o. c., p. 211.

[8] Pont. Com., 23 June, 1918—*A. A. S.*, X (1918), 347.

[9] Sole, o. c., n. 450; Turner, *l. c.*; Ayrinhac, *Penal Legislation*, 364, 2.

[10] Canon 5.

The violation must be in *a notable matter*. Just what this notable matter might be is not easy to determine. Certainly if the violation is not sufficiently grave to constitute the matter of mortal sin it is not amenable to the penalties of this canon.[11] Yet every violation of the common life in a notable matter may not be a mortal sin against the vow of poverty. Of course if the constitutions expressly set forth what a notable matter is there is no difficulty, and as Turner says anything noted in the constitutions as a *graver fault* or subject to graver penalties may be regarded as notable matter.[12]

This is not an altogether certain norm, for as pointed out, all these graver faults are not by that fact mortal sins, and so amenable to punishment.[13]

If the offense is not certain, and even after formal investigation remains only probable, an admonition should be given, if not in virtue of Canon 2389 at any rate in virtue of Canon 2307. Turner[14] holds that the Ordinary *may* give such an admonition. Rather he should say he *must* give it for the canon uses the jussive subjunctive *"moneat"* and is, therefore, perceptive.[15] Turner then goes on to say that this admonition would not suffice for the one prescribed before the infliction of the penalties in Canon 2389, because this canon "expressly declares" that an admonition must be given to a religious who has been guilty of the offense, and hence until the fact of that offense is certainly established judicially, the admonition of 2389 is not to be given. An admonition given previously is not in virtue of Canon 2389, and a religious has the right to admonition in virtue of Canon 2389 before the penalty of privation of active and passive voice or the deposition of a superior is inflicted.[16]

[11] Canon 2218, § 2.

[12] Turner, o. c., p. 212, I, 9, *Constitutiones Sacri Ordinis Praedicatorum* (1932), nn. 905, 906. All the offenses enumerated in n. 906 are certainly material mortal sins, with the exception of the two under consideration; receiving or hiding gifts. In this case according to the universal opinion in the Order, these sins are only grave when the thing received or concealed is grave matter.

[13] Canon 2218, § 2.

[14] Turner, p. 213.

[15] Canon 2307.

[16] Turner, p. 214.

Due weight cannot be denied to this argument, nor does the fact of admonition in virtue of Canon 2307 invalidate it; hence the conclusion can be admitted as more probable, especially in view of present penal jurisprudence.

The admonition in virtue of Canon 2389 becomes preceptive as soon as it is evident either from juridical proof or notoriety of fact [17] that a true crime or delict against the common life has been committed. The term "gravely admonished" certainly seems to point to a public admonition with all due solemnity.[18] The person on whom the obligation of giving the admonition falls is the major superior in exempt institutes or the local ordinary in those non-exempt, either personally or through a delegate, usually the one who has conducted the investigation.[19] The admonition should be given before a notary or two witnesses, or by registered letter and a record of it kept in the secret archives of the Curia.[20]

If after this admonition the religious either continues in the same delict or immediately falls into another of the same kind the privation of active and passive voice and removal of superiors become mandatory as soon as the facts have been proven. If the new offense is not committed till after a long interval, amendment and later relapse is apparent and a new admonition should be given.

The penalty is, of course, *ferendae sententiae* and preceptive, hence, subject to the prescriptions of Canon 2223, § 3, explained above.[21]

---

[17] Canons 2197, 1°, and 1747, 1°.

[18] Canon 2309.

[19] Turner, p. 215. Public admonition is a jurisdictional act.

[20] Canon 2309, §§ 2 and 5. It may be given extra-judicially by way of precept. Canon 1933, § 4.

[21] Supra. Chap. II, Art. 2.

## THE ABUSE OF POWER BY RELIGIOUS SUPERIORS IN GENERAL

### CHAPTER XII

### REGARDING THE ORDINATION OF RELIGIOUS

#### Canon 2410

**Canon 2410.  Superiores Religiosi qui, contra praescriptum Canons 965-967 subditos suos ad Episcopum alienum ordinandos remittere praesumpserint, ipso facto suspensi sunt per mensem a Missal celebratione.***

This canon is from the nature of things very limited in its scope, applying only to major superiors in clerical exempt institutes, who alone, saving extraordinary privilege, have the right to issue dismissorial letters,[1] and to those other superiors who may have this privilege even though they may be members of societies without vows.[2]

Unless the institute enjoys a special privilege in the matter, all religious, even though exempt, must be ordained by the bishop of the diocese in which the religious house to which they are assigned is situated.[3]  They can only be sent to another bishop when the bishop of that diocese gives permission, is of a different rite, or absent, or not to have an ordination on the next regular ordination day, or, finally, if, the see being vacant, the administrator has not the episcopal character.[4]  Moreover, the religious superiors are expressly forbidden [5] to transfer their subjects to a house in another diocese in

---

* Canon 2410.  Religious superiors who, in violation of the prescription of Canons 965-967 presume to send their subjects to another bishop for ordination, are *ipso facto* suspended for one month from the celebration of Mass.

[1] Canon 64, nn. 2°, 4°.

[2] Pont. Com., 2, 3 June, 1918—*A. A. S.* (1918), 347.

[3] Canon 965.

[4] Canon 966.

[5] Canon 967.

order to defraud the bishop of his right to ordain, or to purposely set their ordinations for a time when he is either not having ordinations or is absent. It should be noted that the prescriptions are against defrauding the bishop by these acts; consequently, if the bishop gives his consent to such a transfer or scheduling of the ordination, or if it is done merely to avoid undue delay, the law is not violated nor the penalty incurred.[6] The prescriptions of these canons refer to ordinations to both major and minor orders and even to first tonsure.[7]

The offense punished in this canon is simply the one herein laid down, namely, the sending of a subject, by the issuance of dismissorial letters, to another bishop in violation of the aforesaid canons. Thus, the issuance of invalid dismissorials, as for one who is not a subject or by one who has no power to issue them, even though it be to an alien bishop or accompanied with the fraudulent transfer or setting of time does not constitute the offense nor, therefore, incur the penalty, as the canons cited deal exclusively with valid dismissorials.[8] On the other hand, the offense is consummated by the issuance of the letters or transfer to the other diocese, and hence, the penalty is incurred even though the ordination does not take place.[9] This seems certain inasmuch as it is the *sending* of the candidate to the other bishop which is herein punished. Moreover it is likely that the bishop would refuse to ordain the religious so as not to incur the penalty of canon 2373, n. 4°. This would hardly excuse the religious superior from the penalty, as his offense would have been committed.

The penalty for violation of these prescriptions is *ipso facto* suspension from the celebration of Mass for one month. This, and this alone. The superiors thus suspended remain in the full exercise of their office and may licitly receive or administer the Sacraments and Sacramentals.[10] This penalty is obviously vindictive [11] inasmuch as the time of its duration is specified and its remission

---

[6] Vermeersch-Creusen, *Epitome*, III, n. 615, II.

[7] Canon 950.

[8] Cappello, *De Censuris*, n. 562, 1.

[9] Blat, *Commentarium*, "De Delictis et Poenis," V, n. 256.

[10] Cappello, o. c., n. 563; Blat, *l. c.*

[11] Canon 2286.

does not depend on the cessation of contumacy on the part of the delinquent, and the month, moreover, is to be reckoned from moment to moment as it is in the calendar.[12]   It is also *latae sententiae* with presumption required for incurring it, hence, anything that in any way diminishes the imputability, whether it be on the part of the intellect or of the will, as ignorance, even crass or supine but not affected, error, fear, even though only relatively grave, excuses from the penalty[13]

The question arises as to how this penalty may be remitted before the expiration of the month.   Most of the authors do not treat the question explicitly, but Woywod [14] states clearly that "it cannot be remitted by an authority inferior to the Holy See."   On the other hand, Cipollini [15] holds that since the suspension is not reserved "the dispensation or rather the suspension of the penalty until the month has elapsed is committed to every confessor in the sacramental forum."   And he argues that since in virtue of Canon 2237 the ordinary can dispense from *latae sententiae* penalties of the common law, he can delegate this power to confessors to use in his own favor.

The truth seems somewhere outside these two.   Certainly it is not reserved.   A vindictive penalty may be dispensed according to Canon 2236.[16]   But Canon 2237 also treats of remission of penalties and in the Title (VII) under which it is found there is no distinction between medicinal and vindictive penalties, and 2237 can be applied to this case.[17]   According to this canon the ordinary,[18] which includes major superiors of exempt clerical institutes, may remit *latae sententiae* penalties, except those enumerated in the canon itself, amongst which this suspension is not found.   This power is ordinary

---

[12] Canon 34, § 2.

[13] Canon 2229, § 2.                    ,

[14] Woywod, S., *A Practical Commentary on the Code of Canon Law* (New York, 1932), Vol. II, n. 2236.

[15] Cipollini, *De Censuris*, n. 128.

[16] Canon 2289.

[17] Ayrinhac, *Penal Legislation*, n. 157; Blat, *Commentarium*, "De Delictis et Poenis," V, n. 119.

[18] Canon 198, § 1.

inasmuch as it is annexed to the office by law,[19] and can be delegated inasmuch as it is not expressly forbidden by law.[20]  However, a confessor as confessor has nothing to do with the case unless the case be occult and comes under Canon 2290, which from the nature of this case is difficult to conceive.  The confessor's faculties as such are limited to the internal forum.  Vindictive penalties *per se* pertain to the external forum.  The only concession of jurisdiction regarding them made to confessors by the Code is that of Canon 2290 which applies to more urgent occult cases where the guilty party is exposed to loss of good name and scandal by observance of the penalty.  A prelate may, however be dispensed from the penalty of this canon by dispensation of his own delegates as explained above.

[19] Canon 197.
[20] Canon 199, § 1.

# CHAPTER XIII

## REGARDING ADMISSION OF CANDIDATES TO NOVITIATE AND PROFESSION

### Canon 2411

**Canon 2411. Superiores religiosi qui candidatum non idoneum contra praescriptum Canon 542, aut sine requisitis letteris testimonialibus contra praescriptum Canon 544 ad novitiatum receperint, vel ad professionem contra praescriptum Canon 571, § 2, admiserint, pro gravitate culpae puniantur, non exclusa officii privatione.***

As can be easily understood, the Church must be very careful in regard to the character and quality of persons whom she admits to assume the obligations and enjoy the privileges of the religious state, and it is, therefore, necessary that she lay down in her general law certain qualifications required of everyone who seeks to embrace the religious life. Having carefully laid down these prerequisites it is but natural that she should enforce them with penalties levelled against those who contravene them, and admit unfit candidates in defiance of them.

The penalty of this canon is directed against "religious superiors" but though a general term is used, the nature of the case requires that it applies only to those superiors who have the right to admit candidates to the novitiate and to profession, namely, major superiors.[1] Who these major superiors are is explicitly laid down in

---

*Canon 2411. The religious superiors who will have received to the novitiate an unsuitable candidate contrary to the prescription of Canon 542, or without the requisite testimonial letters contrary to the prescription of Canon 544, or who will have admitted a novice to profession contrary to the prescription of Canon 571, § 2, shall be punished according to the gravity of their fault, even to the extent of being deposed from office. (Authorised English Translation.)

[1] Canon 543.

the Code,[2] namely, the abbot primate, abbot superior of a monastic congregation, abbot of an independent monastery, even though it be part of a monastic congregation, the superior-general of the whole institute, provincial superiors and their vicars, and all who have powers equivalent to those of provincials. Which of these has the right of admitting to the novitiate or to profession, and thus is liable to this penalty, depends on the particular constitutions. It applies, however, to all religious institutes, clerical or lay, of men or of women, exempt or non-exempt, with solemn or simple vows, pontifical or diocesan, and as regards the novitiate even to clerical societies without vows.[3] Blat[4] excludes institutes of nuns subject to the local ordinary and diocesan congregations on the ground that in these institutes the local ordinary alone has the right to admit to the novitiate and to profession.[5] This was true before the Code, but according to the common opinion of the authors[6] and what seems to be the clear prescriptions of the Code, the law has been changed, and major superiors in all institutes have the right in question. Local ordinaries are, nowhere considered as major religious superiors.[7] Hence, the only right they have in admission of candidates is that of examining into their dispositions and free status in institutes of women, expressly granted by the Code,[8] and that which may be granted by particular constitutions.

Those unfit for admission to the noviate according to the prescription of Canon 542 are those whose admission would be invalid, and those whose admission is merely illicit. To the former class belong: [9]

[2] Canon, 488 n. 8.

[3] Pont. Com., 2, 3 June, 1918—A. A. S., X (1918), 347.

[4] Blat, *Commentarium*, "De Delictis et Poenis," V, n. 257.

[5] *Ibid., op. cit.*, "*De Personis*," II, n. 644.

[6] Schäfer, *De Religiosis*, n. 223; Fanfani, *De Jure Reg.*, n. 194; Vermeersch-Creusen, *Epitome* (5th ed.), Vol. I, n. 690; Woywod, *Practical Commentary*, n. 440; Bakalarczyk, R., *De Novitiatu* (Washington, 1927), p. 79; Frey, W. N., *The Act of Religious Profession* (Washington, 1931), pp. 87, 88.

[7] Canon 504 requires that religious superior be a professed religious of the institute.

[8] Canon 552, § 2.

[9] Canon 542, n. 1°.

Those who have adhered to a non-Catholic sect; meaning those who having been baptized Catholics, later fell away and joined a non-Catholic sect. The non-Catholic sect need not be a Christian sect. It may be any sort of non-Catholic religious or irreligious association, Christian, Jewish, Mohammedan, pagan, atheistic, as was expressly declared by the Holy See.[10] Needless to say the persons spoken of here must have repented and returned to the Church, but they are still ineligible for admission to religion.

Those who have not attained the required age, that is, completed their fifteenth year;

Those who enter religion under the influence of violence, grave fear, or fraud, and also those whom the superior receives under pressure of the same influences;

Married persons as long as the marriage bond exists;

Those who are or have been bound by the bonds of religious profession—temporary or perpetual, simple or solemn;

Those who are menaced with punishment for the commission of a grave crime of which they have been or can be accused. In this regard it should be noted that the grave crime must be public but may be against either canon or civil law, and that mere guilt of such a crime does not constitute the impediment. Hence, if one has already fulfilled the penalty or it has been outlawed by the statute of limitations the impediment does not exist.[11]

Every bishop, whether residential or titular, even though only nominated by the Roman Pontiff and not yet consecrated. Hence, not prefects apostolic, prelates inferior to bishops, nor even, under this head, cardinals of the Roman Church who lack the episcopal character.

Clerics who, by a disposition of the Holy See, are bound by oath to consecrate themselves to the service of their diocese or the missions, for the period during which their oath binds them.

To the second class, namely, those whose unfitness renders their admission to the novitiate merely illicit though valid, belong.[12]

---

[10] Pont. Com., 16 October, 1919, and 30 July, 1934—A. A. S., XI (1919), 477, and XXVI (1934), 494.

[11] *Cf.* Bakalarczyk, p. 65.

[12] Canon 542, n. 2°.

Clerics in sacred orders—therefore, not seminarians below the rank of subdeacon, without the consent of the local ordinary or against his will if his objection is based on the serious loss to souls that their withdrawal would import, when that loss cannot by any means be otherwise avoided. If, therefore, the ordinary refuses his consent for any other reason he acts illicitly, the subject is not bound by his refusal and may be licitly admitted to the novitiate.

Those who are burdened with debts which they are unable to discharge;

Those who are liable to furnish accounts or are implicated in other secular negotiations from which the institute may have reason to fear lawsuits and annoyances; which offices may be either of a public or private nature, as long as they may give rise to lawsuits.

Persons whose parents, that is, father or mother, grandfather or grandmother, are in great necessity and need their assistance, and parents whose help is necessary for the maintenance and education of their children;

Those who in religion would be destined for the priesthood, from which, however, they are debarred by an irregularity [13] or other canonical impediment.[14]

Consequently, the superiors who admit to the novitiate a candidate for whom they foresee they will have to obtain a dispensation before he can be ordained, transgress the prescriptions of Canon 542 and are liable to the penalties of Canon 2411. An exception, however, must be made for the case in which the irregularity is taken away by admission to the novitiate or to profession, as in the case of illegitimacy for which the irregularity is removed by solemn profession,[15] and probably, also, according to Vermeersch and others, if the impediment or irregularity will have ceased before ordination.[16] Vermeersch's opinion seems conformable to the common practice and should, therefore, be admitted.

Finally, members of Oriental rites cannot be received in institutes of the Latin rite without written permission

---

[13] Canons 984, 985.

[14] Canon 987.

[15] Canon 984, n. 1.

[16] Vermeersch-Creusen, *Epitome* (5th ed.), Vol. I, n. 686; Fanfani, *De Jure Rel.*, n. 180, 6°; Bakalarczyk, o. c., p. 75.

of the Sacred Congregation for the Oriental Church, except this be for the purpose of preparing themselves to establish religious houses and provinces of their own Oriental rite.[17]

The testimonial letters prescribed in Canon 544 are:

§ 1.  Certificates of baptism and confirmation.

§ 2.  In the case of men, testimonial letters from the ordinary of their birthplace, and the ordinaries of every other place in which they have lived for more than one morally continuous year after having attained their fourteenth year.

§ 3.  When the candidate has been in a seminary, college, or in a postulancy or novitiate of another institute, testimonial letters given according to the circumstances and sworn to [18] by the rector of the seminary or college after consulting the local ordinary, or by the major superior of the institute.  It should be noted here that the term "college" is restricted to ecclesiastical colleges according to the unanimous opinion of the authors and the decrees of the Holy See.[19]

§ 4.  For the admission of clerics it suffices, besides the certificate of ordination, to have testimonial letters from the ordinaries of the dioceses in which the clerics have lived for more than one morally continuous year after ordination, but if they have since ordination attended any other seminary or college, or been admitted to any other postulancy or novitiate he must, likewise, have the sworn letters prescribed in § 3.

§ 5.  For a professed religious passing, by virtue of an apostolic indult, to another institute, the testimony of the major superior of the institute which he leaves suffices.

§ 6.  Besides these testimonies required by law the superiors who have the right of admitting candidates may demand any others that seem necessary or opportune.

§ 7.  Finally, women are not to be admitted until particularly careful investigation has been made regarding their character and conduct, safeguarding the prescriptions of § 3 concerning those who have been in a postulancy or novitiate.

---

[17] Pont. Com., 10 November, 1925, n.—*A. A. S.*, XVII (1925), 583.

[18] Canon 545, § 1.

[19] S. C. de Rel., 4 January and 5 April, 1910—*A. A. S.*, II (1910), 36, 231, 232.

The superior of the institute to which the candidate seeks admission must have these testimonials before he admits him, under the penalties of Canon 2411. On the other hand, the superior whose duty it is to give the letters must either give them within three months or notify the Holy See within that time that he cannot comply, for grave reasons to be explained in this notification,[20] under similar penalties as those in Canon 2411 to be inflicted by the local ordinary in diocesan or lay institutes, or the supreme superior in clerical institutes or religious orders. These penalties, too, may include deposition from office.[21]

The prescription of Canon 571, § 2, is that when the novitiate is completed the novice shall be admitted to profession if he is judged suitable, otherwise he shall be dismissed; but if there arises a doubt regarding his suitability, the higher superiors can prolong the time of probation, but not beyond six months.

The unsuitability referred to here seems to be more extensive than that mentioned in regard to admission to the novitiate. There the prescription of Canon 542 simply enumerated the diriment and prohibitive impediments, and the offense was admitting a person bound by one or more of those. Here the offense is not only admitting those bound by impediments, but anyone who is in any way unfit. The institute has had at least a year to judge from observation the fitness of the novice, and the vote of the chapter or council in that regard is deliberative. If the superior, therefore, admits a novice whom the council or chapter has declared unsuitable, he not only acts invalidly,[22] but becomes liable to the penalties of Canon 2411. Likewise, if notwithstanding a favorable vote by the council or chapter, he has certain knowledge of a candidate's unfitness he, likewise, becomes liable to them if he admits him.

Finally, any major superior who admits a postulant bound by any impediment enumerated above, or without any of the letters also enumerated above, or a novice who is in any way unsuitable, must be punished, by the supreme moderator, or the local ordinary,

[20] Canon 545, §§ 1 and 2.

[21] S. C. de Rel., 21 November, 1919—*A. A. S.*, XII (1926), 17.

[22] Canon 105, n. 1°.

if the culprit be the superior general of a lay or diocesan institute, according to the gravity of the fault, considered quantitatively or qualitatively, even to the extent of being deprived of office.   It is an indetermined, *ferendae sententiae* penalty, the infliction of which is preceptive, and, therefore, subject to the regulations of Canon 2223, § 3.

# CHAPTER XIV

## INTERFERENCE WITH CANONICAL VISITATION

Canon 2413

Canon 2413, § 1.  Antistitae quae post indictam visitationem religiosas in aliam domum, Visitatore non consentiente, transtulerint, itemque religiosae omnes, sive antistitae sie subditae, quae per se vel per alios, directe vel indirecte, religiosas induxerint ut interrogatae a Visitatore taceant vel veritatem quoquo modo dissimulent aut non sincere exponant, vel eisdem, ob responsa quae Visitatori dederint, molestiam, sub quovis praetextu, attulerint, inhabiles ad officia assequenda, quae aliarum regimen secumferunt, a Visitatore declarentur et antistitae officio, quo funguntur, priventur.

§ 2.  Quae in superiore paragrapho praescripta sunt, etiam virorum religionibus applicentur.*

THE law regarding visitations is laid down in Canons 511, 512, and 513.  Major superiors designated to do so must visit all the houses subject to them, either personally or through a delegate, at the times laid down in the particular constitutions.  Likewise, the local ordinary must visit every five years, either in person or through a

---

* Canon 2413, § 1.  Superioresses who, after the visitation has been announced, will have transferred religious to another house, without the consent of the Visitator, likewise, all the religious, whether superioresses or subjects, who, personally or through others, directly or indirectly, will have induced any religious not to reply to the questions of the Visitator, or to dissimulate or not sincerely expose the truth, and, finally, those who, under whatever pretext will have molested any religious on account of replies which she may have given to the Visitator, shall be declared by the Visitator as incapable of obtaining any office which bears with it the government of other religious, and the superioresses, if found guilty in this respect, shall be deposed from office.

§ 2.  The prescriptions of the preceding paragraph are also applicable to the institutes of men.  (Authorised English Translation.)

delegate, the institutes and institutions specified in the law.[1] The visitator has the right and duty to interrogate the religious whom he deems it well to hear and inform himself about those things which come within the scope of the visitation: orthodox doctrine, sound morals, exact discipline, good religious spirit, efficient administration of temporalities, liturgical correctness.[2] The religious are under obligation of replying truthfully, and neither superiors nor others may lawfully divert them from this obligation or impede the visitation.[3] Violation of these laws is punished by Canon 2413.

Three offenses are considered in this canon.

1. The illicit transfer of a religious to another house without the visitator's consent.

2. The inducing of religious to conceal or dissimulate the truth before the visitator.

3. Molesting a religious on account of the responses she has given to the visitator.

The first can be committed by superiors alone; the other two by subjects also.

1. The general term superioresses applies to all without distinction, both major and local, and in virtue of the second paragraph it applies also to men, not only in religious institutes, but in clerical societies without vows.[4] These superioresses or superiors, as the case may be, are forbidden to transfer a religious from one house to another after the forthcoming visitation of the former house has been announced. What form the transfer may take is of no importance. It may be the formal assignment by a provincial, for example, in view of a visitation by the general, or it may be a temporary mission coming from the local superior after the announcement of the visitation by provincial, general, or local ordinary. If real necessity suddenly arises after the announcement of the visitation, a transfer is not prohibited, but the consent of the visitator must be obtained. It seems superfluous to mention that the transfer

---

[1] Canon 512.

[2] Sole, *De Delictis et Poenis,* n. 479.

[3] Canon 513.

[4] Pont. Com., 2, 3 June, 1918—*A. A. S.,* X (1918), 347.

of a subject by the provincial or general after the announcement of a coming visitation by the respective delegate of either is not forbidden or punished, for the prelate's command more than supplies his own delegate's consent. Moreover, the transfer of a religious with knowledge of an announcement of visitation to be made, but before the announcement is made, does not constitute the offense nor incur the penalty of this canon.[5]

2. Both superiors and subjects are forbidden to induce other religious, in any way whatsoever, directly or indirectly, personally or through others, not to answer, or not to answer truthfully the questions asked by the visitator. The questions of course must be those falling within the scope of the visitation. What pertains exclusively to the internal forum is no affair of the visitator, nor should he or she inquire about it, and if she does the subject is not bound to answer and may be so instructed by the local superior or others without incurring this penalty. For example, if a visitator asks a sister if, and how often, she has made use of the privilege of Canon 522 regarding an occasional confessor, she not only exceeds her power but makes herself liable to the penalties of Canon 2414, and the sister need not respond. A superior or subject who advises another sister of this fact does not incur the penalties of this canon.

However, when the question is legitimate it must be answered directly, and truthfully, without any dissimulation, equivocation, ambiguity or the like and anyone who induces a religious to respond otherwise commits the offense herein punished. It would seem that the effect must be produced, that is, that the religious interrogated must really have dissimulated in some way as the result of the urging; otherwise the culprits would have "attempted to induce" rather than have "induced" her to this dissimulation.

It should be noted, too, that "clearly exposing the truth" must be moderated with charity and prudence as Creusen remarks, and the defects of individual religious, or occult sins, or faults, even grave, of superiors, unless these constitute a real menace to the good order or morality of the community, should not be mentioned unless

---

[5] Blat, *Commentarium*, "De Delictis et Poenis," V, n. 259.

asked.[6]  To inform subjects of this fact is not a violation of this canon, but it should be left to the confessor.

Finally, all those who will have molested in any way and under any pretext whatsoever any religious on account of the replies given in visitation, fall under the penalties of this canon.  This applies to all, whether superiors or subjects, and the term used, molestation, is of the broadest extent.  Any noticeable coolness towards or annoyance given to the victim, any favoritism shown against her, unusual harshness particularly in imposing penances or distribution of assignments, come under this law.  Of course they must be the result of the responses given in visitation, and not because of other and independent motives, but such extrinsic motives must not be mere pretexts, otherwise the law is broken and the penalty incurred.  Even if the religious has wounded charity or prudence she is not to be molested therefor,[7] but if the testimony is false this fact should be manifested to the visitator or his superior and the punishment left up to them.

The penalty for these three offenses is the same.  Those guilty are to be declared incapable of holding office which bears with it the government of other religious.  Office here must be taken in the broad sense as is evident from the context,[8] for it deals primarily with women who cannot participate in the power of orders or jurisdiction.  However, it does not take in all offices, but only those to which is annexed the government of other religious—hence, not such as syndic, librarian, etc.

The penalty is inflicted by the mere fact of its declaration by the visitator, without any judicial process, but the offense must of course be certain.

Superiors, if they be guilty, are, moreover, to be deposed from the office which they hold.  This removal is, from the wording of the canon, to be effected by the visitator, in the same manner as the other penalties are to be imposed by him, namely, by particular decree.

---

[6] Vermeersch-Creusen, *Epitome* (4th ed.), Vol. III, n. 816, 2°.

[7] *Ibid., l. c.*

[8] Canon 145; also Blat, *Commentarium*, V, n. 259.

The penalties are *ferendae sententiae* but their infliction preceptive and hence, the prescriptions of Canon 2223, § 3, apply.

The second paragraph was necessary because although according to Canon 490 the masculine form applied also to institutes of women, the converse could not be invoked in a penal law requiring strict interpretation, otherwise it would be an extension of penalty from person to person forbidden by Canon 2219, § 3.

## SECTION IV

## THE ABUSE OF POWER BY SUPERIORESSES IN PARTICULAR

### CHAPTER XV

### REGARDING DOWRIES AND NOTIFICATION TO LOCAL ORDINARY OF RECEPTION OR PROFESSION

CANON 2412

**Canon 2412. Religiosarum etiam exemptarum antis-titae pro gravitate culpae, non exclusa, si res ferat, officii privatione, ab Ordinario loci puniantur.**

**1° Si contra praescriptum Canon 549 dotes puellarum receptarum quoquo modo impendere praesumpserint, salva semper obligatione de qua in Canon 551.***

ARTICLE 1.  DOWRIES

THE dowry or deposit of a fixed and substantial sum of money is required of all postulants in monasteries of nuns before reception of the habit, and in other institutes of women the constitutions concerning it are to be followed exactly, the Holy See alone having power to dispense with it in whole or in part in Pontifical institutes, the local ordinary in diocesan congregations.  The sum is fixed by constitutions or lawful custom.[1]  This dowry is to be held by the institute during the novitiate and after the first profession the

---

* Canon 2412.  The superioresses even of exempt religious women shall be punished by the local ordinary according to the gravity of their fault, including, if necessary, even deposition from office.

1°. If, contrary to the prescription of Canon 549, they will have presumed to spend, in whatever manner, the dowries of the young girls received into the institute, always safeguarding the obligation mentioned in Canon 551. (Authorised English Translation.)

[1] Canon 547.

mother-general or mother-provincial, with her council and with the consent of the local ordinary, and if the house be subject to regulars with the consent of the regular superior also, must place it in a safe, lawful and productive investment, but it is strictly forbidden to spend any part of the dowry for any purpose whatsoever, even for building a new house or liquidating debts during the lifetime of the religious,[2] though the institute may use the fruits of and interest accruing from the investment of the dowry during that time.[3]   On the death of the religious the dowry is irrevocably acquired by the monastery even though she had made profession of only temporary vows,[4] but if she leaves the institute, from whatever cause, the dowry must be returned [5] intact.   If, however, by virtue of an apostolic indult, the professed religious joins another institute the interest on the dowry during her new novitiate, and after profession the dowry itself must be given to her new institute; but if she merely passes from one monastery to another of the same order, the dowry is due the latter from the day the change takes place.[6]

The penalty in this canon is leveled at those superioresses who presume, in defiance of the prohibition, to spend the principal of the dowry during the lifetime of sisters who brought it, for any cause whatsoever, no matter how useful or even necessary it may seem. Only the Holy See can permit an exception in this matter, and it is very slow to do so.  As Vermeersch says, "Even here urgent cases may arise where this principle holds: 'necessity knows no law.' "  But in such case the dowry must be reconstructed as soon as possible.[7]

The term, "superioresses of religious women," is most sweeping and includes all superioresses, general, provincial, or local, of all institutes of women, whether Pontifical or diocesan, of simple or solemn vows, and even though they be exempt, as is expressly added. The laws regarding dowries is more strict for nuns than for sisters, but the penal law against spending their dowries weighs with equal

---

[2] Canon 549.

[3] Schäfer, n. 232.

[4] Canon 548.

[5] Canon 551, § 1.

[6] Canon 551, § 2.

[7] Vermeersch-Creusen, *Epitome,* Vol. I (5th ed.), n. 669.

force on superioresses of both. From the nature of this case of the dowries, however, the penalty affects only major superiors, as they alone have charge of the dowries or are in a position to expend them.[8]

This Canon, 2412, contains the term, "will have presumed," but strictly speaking, this phrase is not here regulated by Canon 2229, which applies expressly to *latae sententiae* penalties. The penalty of this canon is *ferendae sententiae*. However, since it is not a case of drawing a penalty from case to case, the interpretation from parallel places of the Code[9] may be invoked, and it may be admitted that any diminution of the culpability, even through crass ignorance, excuses from the penalty.[10]

### Article 2. Notification to Local Ordinary of Reception and Profession

#### Canon 2412, 2°

**Canon 2412, 2°. Si contra praescriptum Canon 552 omiserint Ordinarium loci certiorem facere de proxima alicujus admissione ad novitiatum vel ad professionem.***

The prescription of Canon 552, which is taken from the decree of the Council of Trent[11] ordains that the local ordinary or a priest delegated by him, must, at least thirty days before the admission of a woman to the novitiate, and to profession both of temporary and perpetual or simple and solemn vows, carefully examine the dispositions of the aspirant and inform himself as to whether she has been constrained or beguiled, and if she understands the import of the step she is about to take, and he must assure himself of her pious intention and freedom of action. In order that this examination

---

[8] Canon 550, § 1.

[9] Canon 18.

[10] Blat, *Commentarium*, "De Delictis et Poenis," V, n. 258; Chelodi, *Jus Poenale*, n. 113, 2.

* Canon 2412, 2°. If, contrary to the prescription of Canon 552, they will have omitted to inform the local ordinary concerning the approaching admission of a subject to the novitiate or to profession. (Authorised English Translation.)

[11] Conc. Trid., Sess. XXV, *de regularibus*, c. 17.

may take place, the first paragraph of the canon directs that the superioress, even of exempt religious, must inform the local ordinary at least two months in advance of the approaching admission to the novitiate and to the profession, both of temporary and perpetual, or of simple and solemn vows. The temporary profession here mentioned is the first profession, and not renewal of temporary vows, so that according to what Pruemmer rightly calls the more true opinion, this examination is to take place but three times: before reception, before first profession, before final profession.[12]

The superioress on whom the duty of notifying the ordinary falls, and consequently, the one who incurs the penalty if she neglects this duty, is she whom the constitutions designate. It may be the general or provincial superior, or the superior of the novitiate house, but if the constitutions do not determine the point it naturally falls on her whose right it is to admit to reception or profession, that is, the major superior.[13] Once she has notified the ordinary in time, she has no more responsibility in the matter, nor can she be held culpable if the examination is omitted, or if the admission takes place without it.[14]

This part of the canon does not contain the term "presume," and, consequently, the prescription of Canon 2229, § 2, about crass and supine ignorance cannot be applied even by extension. It is up to the local ordinary to consider such things in punishing "according to the gravity of the offense." However, as Chelodi justly remarks the crime, and, consequently, the penalty, would not be had unless there were malice or grave negligence involved.[15]

Under the old law the penalty was not incurred if the reception or profession did not take place.[16] This was in regard to the penalty decreed by the Council of Trent [17] for failure to notify the bishop a

---

[12] Pruemmer, *Man. J. C.*, n. 207, 2; Fanfani, *De Jure Rel.*, n. 246c; Vermeersch-Creusen, *Epitome*, I (5th ed.), n. 703.

[13] Vermeersch-Creusen, *Epitome*, I, n. 703.

[14] *Ibid., l. c.*

[15] Chelodi, *Jus Poenale*, n. 113, 2.

[16] S. C. Conc., *Brundusina*, 27 February, 1610—*Fontes*, n. 2385.

[17] Conc. Trid., Sess. XXV, *de regularibus*, c. 17.

month before the reception or profession.  The penalty was suspension from office.  Though no author seems to hold that the decision of 1610 applies to Canon 2412, it would seem that in virtue of Canon 6, 3°, that it still should hold.  This law is partly in conformity with the old law, and should, therefore, be judged in that part from the old law.  But the part which is in conformity is the very part affected by the decision in question, namely, the substance of the offense: Did failure to notify constitute the offense in case the reception or profession failed to take place?  Certainly this conformity should at least give rise to a doubt as to whether or not the decision holds, and in case of doubt the old law is not to be given up.[18]  Nor does Canon 6, 5°, stand in the way.  True, it says, "What pertains to penalties," but its obvious meaning is that penalties themselves, not contained in the Code, are abrogated, and does not mean that an interpretation of an offense is necessarily abrogated also.

Finally, the penalty for the offenses treated in both articles of this chapter is punishment by the local ordinary, according to the gravity of the fault, even to the extent of deprivation of office, if the nature of the case demands it.  The infliction of the penalty is preceptive, though the penalty is undetermined; hence, the prescriptions of Canon 2209 apply.  The crimes, of course, must be certain; but judicial proof is not necessary and the bishop will ordinarily act administratively, or by way of precept in imposing the penalty.

[18] Canon 6, n. 4.

# CHAPTER XVI

## INTERFERENCE WITH THE LIBERTY OF CONFESSION

Canon 2414

**Canon 2414.  Antistita quae contra praescriptum Canon 521, § 3, 522, 523, se gesserit, a loci Ordinario moneatur; si iterum deliquerit, ab eodem officii privatione puniatur, illico tamen certiore facta Sacra Congregatione de Religiosis.**[*]

THIS last canon of the Code applies to all superioresses without exception, prescribing against them the penalty of removal from office if they interfere with the liberty of conscience conceded to their subjects by the prescriptions of the canons mentioned.  The matter of liberty of conscience is so grave, that in order to insure against unlawful interference with it, the Church has enacted this grave penalty for such interference.

The law requires that the local ordinaries designate over and above the ordinary and extraordinary confessors for each house of religious women certain other priests, more than one in each case, as supplementary confessors, to whom the religious may easily have recourse for the Sacrament of Penance, and the superioress must provide the confessor requested, if possible, nor can she personally or through others, directly or indirectly, ask to know the reason for the request, show opposition to it by word or deed, or in any way manifest displeasure at it.[1]

Moreover, when a religious for the peace of her conscience has approached an occasional confessor approved by the local ordinary

---

[*] Canon 2414.  If a superioress acts against the prescriptions of Canons 521, § 3, 522, and 523, she shall be admonished by the local ordinary; if again found delinquent she shall be punished by removal from office, and the Sacred Congregation of Religious immediately informed of the matter.  (Authorised English Translation.)

[1] Canon 521, §§ 2 and 3.

to hear the confessions of women, in a place lawfully designated for hearing confessions of women, the superioress may not prohibit it or make any enquiry concerning it, even indirectly.[2]  Finally, she can neither directly nor indirectly prevent religious who are seriously sick, even though not in danger of death, from asking any priest approved for hearing women's confessions to hear their confession as often as they wish.[3]

All agree that this canon should be applied rigorously, in order to terminate abuses in this matter which still exist,[4] but it is first of all necessary to understand clearly just what points do fall under the prescriptions of this law.

The superioress is forbidden under penalty of the sanctions of Canon 2414 to prohibit, impede, or in any way interfere with the use of any of these privileges.  Direct or indirect enquiry, and prohibition regarding it, is forbidden in all three cases,[5] but refusal to call the confessor is punished only in the case of the supplementary confessor and the confessor of the sick.[6]  Showing displeasure is specifically mentioned as an offense in Canon 521, § 2, but is certainly included under indirect prohibition likewise.  It is frequently so difficult to establish the fact in this case that a bishop would hardly care to proceed to removal from office on such uncertain grounds.  However, should the displeasure be shown in unmistakable terms, as for instance, by reprimand, imposition of penance, or the like, he has ample grounds for action.

The law is inflexible on all these points, and no superior, major or minor, may violate it without rendering herself liable to the penal sanctions, no matter what reason she may have.  In the case of abuses arising from the exercise of the rights in question, the most the superioress can do is inform the local ordinary.  If she should impose a penance on a religious for the exercise of any one of these rights

---

[2] Canon 522.

[3] Canon 523.

[4] *Cf.* McCormick, R. E., *Confessors of Religious* (Washington, D. C., 1926), p. 173.

[5] Canon 521, §§ 2 and 3, and Canons 522 and 523.

[6] Canons 521, §§ 2 and 3, and Canon 523; McCormick, p. 229; De Sobradillos, A. M., *De Religiosarum Confesariis* (Turin, 1932), p. 233.

she would offend against the canon by indirectly forbidding its use.

The specific ways in which this law may be broken are too numerous to mention, and examples are superfluous, in view of the clear and extensive terminology of the Code itself. It might be well, however, to point out certain acts which may seem to be, but are not, violations of these prescriptions.

In the first place, the offense herein punished is not committed when the superioress refuses to call an occasional confessor of Canon 522, or when she refuses permission for a sister to leave the convent in order to approach one of them,[7] though in virtue of another decision [8] she is not, as McCormick held [9] under obligation to refuse. Neither does she violate the law if she reprimands or even punishes a subject who has gone out without permission for the purpose of using the privilege of Canon 522. Again, the law is not broken if the superioress reminds a subject apparently remiss in the matter, that she is obliged to frequent the ordinary confessor, and when a religious neglects her weekly confession to the ordinary confessor, even though she has confessed to another, the superioress, far from violating the law, is only fulfilling her duty [10] when she calls the attention of such a one to her obligation of confessing each week. In these latter cases, however, she must be particularly careful that her remarks do not savor of complaint, reprimand or enquiry, and if it be a question of the supplementary, rather than the occasional confessor, she must refrain from any remarks or even gestures.

The violation of this canon carries a preceptive, determined *ferendae sententiae* punishment, namely, canonical admonition for the first offense, and privation of office for the second. The infliction of this penalty is confided now to the local ordinary. The local ordinary in question may be either the ordinary of the place in which the offense was committed,[11] or the ordinary of the place in which

---

[7] S. C. de Rel., 1 December, 1921—Woywod, S., *Canonical Divisions of the Holy See* (New York, 1933), p. 49.

[8] Pont. Com., 28 December, 1927—A. A. S. (1928), 61.

[9] McCormick, *op. cit.*, p. 195.

[10] Canon 595, § 1, n. 3.

[11] Canons 1566, 1579, § 3.

the house to which the offending superioress is assigned is located.[12] This becomes important only in case the offending superioress is a major superioress, with habitual residence outside the place where the offense was committed.

The admonition after the first offense should be given by the ordinary personally, or through another,[13] advisably the chancery or the regular or ecclesiastical superior. Unlike the admonition regarding violation of common life [14] this may be either public or secret,[15] and in fact a secret warning is preferable,[16] but some record of it must be kept in the secret achives of the diocesan Curia.[17] It is true that admonition may be given merely on suspicion, but as was said concerning common life, that does not seem to suffice here. In other words, an admonition is the penalty for the first offense, which must be at least morally certain from notoriety of fact, or as a result of the special inquisition described in Canons 1939-1946, following denunciation.[18] If admonition were given only on suspicion of a first offense it would not be in virtue of this canon. The superioress could not be removed after another offense was proven, as she would still have right to the canonical admonition in virtue of this canon before she could be removed for another offense committed after it.

The denunciation should be made, first of all, by the subject whose right was interfered with, or by any one else having certain knowledge of the offense. Since most of these abuses are secret, the law becomes quite useless without such denunciations. Hence, it would seem that the obligation to make them, either personally or through others, is *per se,* grave, but in the concrete cases, circumstances may excuse from the gravity of the obligation. Nevertheless, the ordinaries ought to watch vigilantly over this matter and strike vigorously at abuses which still arise.

The removal for a second offense need not be by judicial action,

<hr>

[12] Canons 1563, 1579, § 3. *Cf.* Woywood, *Commentary,* Vol. II, n. 1571.
[13] Canon 2307.
[14] Canon 2389.
[15] Canon 2309, § 1.
[16] McCormick, o. c., p. 172.
[17] Canon 2309, § 5.
[18] Canons 2233, § 1, and 1946, § 2, nn. 1°, 3°.

but simply by decree, and the Sacred Congregation of Religious must be notified at once so that, particularly in the case of general or provincial superioress, provision may be made at once.

A vigorous prosecution of offenders by the ordinaries coupled with conscientious coöperation on the part of the religious, who should be taught to realize the gravity of their obligation to do their share in stamping out these abuses, is necessary for the elimination of a particularly odious type of tyranny that still exists in some quarters.

# BIBLIOGRAPHY


#### SOURCES

*Acta Apostolicae Sedis*, Rome, 1909.

*Acta Sanctae Sedis*, 41 vols., Rome, 1865-1908.

*Benedicti P. XIV Bullarium*, 17 vols., Prati, 1845-1846.

Berardi, C. S., *Gratiani Canones Genuini ab Apocryphis Discreti, Corrupti ad emendationum Codicum Fidem Exacti, Difficiliores Commoda Interpretatione Illustrati*, 3 vols. in 4, Venice, 1777.

*Bullarium Romanum*, 24 vols., continuata, 13 vols., Augustae-Taurinorum, 1858-1872.

*Canones et Decreta Concilii Tridentini*, Turin, 1913.

*Codex Juris Canonici*, Rome, 1917.

*Codex Theodosianus* (Mommsen), Berlin, 1903.

*Collectanea Sacrae Congregationes Episcoporum et Regularium* (Bizzari), Rome, 1885.

*Collectanea Sacrae Congregationis de Propaganda Fidei*, 2 vols., Rome, 1907.

*Collectio omnium Conclusionum et Resolutionum Sacrae Congregationis Concilii* (Pallotini), 17 vols., Rome, 1868-1893.

*Corpus Juris Canonici* (Richter-Friedberg), 2 vols., Leipzig.

*Corpus Juris Civilis* (Vol. III, Scholl-Kroll), Berlin, 1912.

Denzinger, H.-Bannwart, C., *Enchiridion Symbolorum Defitionum et Declarationum de rebus Fidei et Morum*, Fribourg, 1922.

*Fontes Codicis Juris Canonici* (Cura Emi. P. Gasparri edita), Rome, 1925.

Hardouin, J., *Act Conciliorum et Epistulae Decretales ac Constitutiones Summorum Pontificum*, 12 vols., Paris, 1714-1725.

Mansi, J. D., *Collectio Amplissima et Novissima Sacrorum Conciliorum*, 53 vols., Paris, 1901-1927.

Migne, J. R., *Patrologia Graeca*, 161 vols., Paris, 1858-1864.

Migne, J. R., *Patrologia Latina*, 221 vols., Paris, 1847-1870.

#### LITERATURE—PRINCIPAL WORKS CONSULTED

Alphonsus Ligouri, St., *Theologia Moralis*, 4 vols., Rome, 1905.

Appletern, Victor ab, *Compendium Praelectionum Juris Regularium*, Adm. R. P. Piati Montensis, Tournai, 1903.

Ayrinhac-Lydon, *Marriage Legislation in the New Code of Canon Law*, New York, 1932.

Ayrinhac, A. S., *Penal Legislation in the New Code of Canon Law*, New York, 1920.

Bachofen, A., *Compendium Juris Regularium*, New York, 1903.

[Bachofen], C. Augustine, *A Commentary on the New Code of Canon Law*, 8 vols., St. Louis, 1918-1922.

Bastien, P., *Directoire Canonique a l'usage des Congregations a Voeux Simples*, 4th ed., Bruges, 1933.

Bakalarczyk, R., *De Novitatu*, Washington, 1927.

Blat, A., *Commentarium in Textum Codicis Juris Canonici*, 6 vols., Rome, 1921-1927.

Bouché, J., in *Dictionnaire de Droit Canonique*, Paris, 1928.

Bouix, D., *Tractatus de Jure Regularium*, 2 vols., Brussels, 1867.

Bouscaren, *Canon Law Digest*, Milwaukee, 1934.

Bouaert-Simenon, *Manuale Juris Canonici*, Ghent, 1924.

*Bullarium Ordinis Praedicatorum*, Rome, 1759.

*Canonical Legislation Concerning Religious* (Authorised English Translation), Rome, 1919.

Cappello, *De Censuris*, Turin, 1933.

Cerato, P., *Censurae Vigentes ipso facto*, Patavia, 1921.

Cerato, P., *Matrimonium a Codice Juris Canonici Integre Desumptum*, Patavia, 1919.

Chelodi, J., *Jus de Personis*, Trent, 1927.

————, *Jus Matrimoniale*, Trent, 1921.

————, *Jus Poenale*, Trent, 1933.

Cicognani, H. J., *Canon Law*, Philadelphia, 1934.

Cipollini, A., *De Censuris Latae Sententiae*, Turin, 1925.

Cocchi, G., *Commentarium in Codicem Juris Canonicis*, 9 vols., Turin, 1924-1927.

Conte a Coronata, M., *Institutiones Juris Canonici*, Turin, 1928.

*Constitutiones Sacri Ordinis Praedicatorum* (Saulchoir), Rome, 1933.

Creusen, J.-Garesché, *Religious Men and Women in Church Law*, Milwaukee, 1931.

Crinica, A., *Modificationes in Tractatu de Censuris per Codicem Juris Canonici Introductae*, S. Mauritii Aguaensis, 1919.

D'Annibale, J. Card., *Summula Theologiae Moralis*, 5th ed., 3 vols., Rome, 1908.

De Meester, A., *Juris Canonici et Juris Canonico Civilis Compendium*, 3 vols., Bruges, 1921-1927.

De Sobradillo, A. M., *De Religiosarum Confessariis*, Turin, 1932.

*Dictionnaire de Droit Canonique*, Paris, 1928.

Eichmann, E., *Lehrbuch des Kirchenrechts*, Paderborn, 1926.

Fanfani, L., *De Jure Religiosorum*, Rome and Turin, 1925.

Gasparri, P. Card., *Tractatus Canonicus de Matrimonio*, 2 vols., Typis Polyglottis Vaticanus, 1932.

Génicot-Salsmans, *Institutiones Theologiae Moralis*, Brussels, 1932.

Goyeneche, S., Consultationes in *Commentarium pro Religiosis*, XI, 1930.

Hefele, J.-Leclercq, *Histoire des Conciles*, 9 vols., Paris, 1907-1930.

Hickey, J., *Irregularities and Simple Impediments in the New Code of Canon Law*, Washington, 1920.

Hippolytus a Sancta Familia, "De Dimissione Religiosorum," *Analecta, O. C. D.*, IV, 1930.

Hollweck, J., *Kirchliche Strafgesetze*, Mainz, 1899.

Hyland, F. E., *Excommunication* (Washington, 1928).

Leduc, A., *De Locis et Temporibus Sacris*, Rome, 1931.

Leduc, A., *De Religiosis*, Rome, 1930.

Leech, G. L., *The Constitution "Apostolicae Sedis" and the "Codex Juris Canonici,"* Washington, 1922.

Lega, M. Card., *De Judiciis Ecclesiasticus*, 4 vols., Rome, 1899.

Leitner, M., *Handbuch des Katolischen Kirchenrechts*, 5 vols., Munschen, 1921-1927.

MacKenzie, E., *The Delict of Heresy*, Washington, 1932.

McCormick, R. E., *The Confessors of Religious*, Washington, 1926.

Michalicka, W. C., *Judicial Procedure in Dismissal of Clerical Exempt Religious*, Washington, 1925.

Noldin, H., *Summa Theologiae Moralis*, 3 vols., Oenipotente, 1922.

Noval, J., *De Processibus*, Rome, 1923.

Ojetti, B., *Synopsis Rerum Moralium et Juris Pontificium*, 4 vols., Rome, 1912.

O'Neill, W., *Papal Rescripts of Favor*, Washington, 1930.

Palombo, J., *De Dimissione Religiosorum*, Turin and Rome, 1931.

Papi, H., *Religious in Church Law*, New York, 1924.

Papi, H., *Religious Profession*, New York, 1918.

Piatus Montennis, *Praelectiones Juris Regularis*, 2 vols., Tournai, 1898.

Pistochi, M., *Canoni Penali*, Tournai, 1925.

Preummer, D., *Manuale Theologiae Moralis*, 3 vols., Fribourg, 1928.

Preummer, D., *Manuale Juris Canonici*, Fribourg, 1927.

Quigley, J. A., *Condemned Societies*, Washington, 1927.

Reiffenstuel, F. A., *Jus Canonicum Universum*, Antwerp, 1743.

Roberti, F., *De Delictis et Poenis*, Rome.

Salucci, R., *Il Diritto Penale*, Subiaco, 1926.

Saucedo, P. R., "Exercitium Jurisdictionis et Superiores Laici ex Ordine Hospitalario S. Joannes de Deo," in *Commentarium pro Religiosis* (XIII), 1932.

Schaaf, V. T., *The Cloister*, Cincinnati, 1921.

Schäfer, T., *De Religiosis*, Münster, 1931.

Simon, J., *Faculties of Pastors and Confessors for Absolution and Dispensation*, New York, 1922.

Smith, S. B., *Elements of Ecclesiastical Law*, Vol. III, "Ecclesiastical Punishments," New York, 1888.

Sole, J., *De Delictis et Poenis*, Rome, 1920.

Steiger, J., "De Vitae Religiosae Propagatione et Diffusione Synopsis Historica," *Periodica de re Canonica* (XIII), Rome, 1924.

Suarez, E., *De Judiciis*, Rome, 1933.

Tabera, A., "De Dimissione Religiosorum," in *Commentarium pro Religiosis* (XI), 1930.

Thomas Aquinas, St., *Summa Theologica*.

Turner, S. J., *The Vow of Poverty*, Washington, 1929.

Vermeersch, A., *De Religiosis*, 2 vols., Bruges, 1907.

Vermeersch-Creusen, *Epitome Juris Canonici*, 3 vols., Brussels, 1930-1933.

Wernz, F. X., *Jus Decretalium*, 6 vols., Prati, 1913.

Wernz-Vidal, *De Religiosis*, Rome, 1932.

Woywod, S., *Canonical Decisions of the Holy See*, New York, 1933.

Woywod, S., *A Practical Commentary on the Code of Canon Law*, 2 vols., New York, 1932.

PERIODICALS

*American Ecclesiastical Review*, Philadelphia, 1889.

*Analecta Ordinis Carmelitarum Excalceatorum*, Rome, 1926.

*Analecta Ordinis Praedicatorum*, Rome, 1892.

*Angelicum*, Rome.

*Apollinaris*, Rome, 1928.

*Commentarium Pro Religiosis*, Rome, 1920.

*Homiletic and Pastoral Monthly*, New York.

*Irish Ecclesiastical Record*, Dublin.

*Jus Pontificium*, Rome, 1921.

*Periodica de Re Canonica et Morali*, Bruges, 1905.

# ALPHABETICAL INDEX


Abuse of Power by superiors,
  Admitting unworthy candidates to novitiate or to profession, 132ff.
  Interfering with liberty of conscience, 149ff.
  Interfering with visitation, 139ff.
  Neglecting to notify Bishop of approaching reception or profession, 146ff.
  Sending subjects to alien Bishop for ordination, 132ff.
  Spending dowries of subjects, 145.
Acts, Legitimate Ecclesiastical, 98, 99.
Admission to novitiate, unfit for, 133-137.
  to profession, 137, 138.
Ancient Law, 3.
Apostolic Delegate, 52.
Apostolic Letters, meaning of, 79.
"*Apostolicae Sedis*," Constitution of Pius IX, 31, 32.
Apostolic See, letters of, 77-79.
  meaning, 79.
Apostates, from the faith, 39ff.
  from religion, 94ff.
Authority, of Roman Pontiff, Papal Legates, Proper Ordinary, crimes against, 51-53.
Bishop, to be notified of approaching reception or Profession of Sisters, 146.
  proper for ordination of religious, 132.
Carbonari, 61.
Care of souls, decision concerning those exercising, 87 footnote.
Clementines, Book of, 19.
Cloister of men, penalties for violation of, 64ff.

of nuns, penalties for violation of, 72ff.
Cluniac reform, 7.
Commercial Trading, penalty against, 84-86.
Common life, definition of, 124.
  penalties for violation of, 127.
Conferences, diocesan; neglect of, 82.
Conspiracy, against Pope, Papal Legate, Proper Ordinary, 51.
Council Artes II, 11.
  of Carthage, 11.
  of Chalcedon, laws from, 4, 5.
  of Elvira, canon of, 12.
  of Lateran I, 7.
  of Lateran II, 7, 8.
  of Lateran III, 14-16.
  of Lyons II, 18.
  of Nicea, 4.
  spurious constitutions of, 3.
  of Orleans I, 11.
  of Orleans V, 12.
  of Paris VI, 10.
  of Toledo IV, 11.
  of Toledo VI, 11.
  of Trent, 21-24.
  of Vienne, 19.
  of Tribur, 12.
*Crimen Falsi*, 76.
Decree of Gratian, 3ff.
Decretals of Gregory IX, 14.
Dismissal of religious, *ipso jure*, 39, 104, 119.
Dismissed religious, restrictions on and penalties against, 87-93.
Dowries, spending of, 145.
Excommunication, reserved *simpliciter* to the Holy See, attempting marriage with solemn vows, 111.

illegitimate egress of nuns from cloister, 72.

reserved to major superior, apostasy from religion in exempt institutes, 94ff.

reserved to ordinary, apostasy from religion in lay and non-exempt institutes, 98.

marriage or attempted marriage of religious with simple perpetual vows, 117.

effect of, 88, 89.

Fenians, 61.

Flight with person of opposite sex, 104-107.

Fraud, invalidating profession, 108ff.

Fugitives, penalties against, 101.

Forgery, 76ff.

Heresy, as distinguished from apostasy, 40ff.

Holy Office, religious joining persons to be denounced to, 59-63.

Holy See, excommunication reserved to, 111.

Infamy of law, 89, 90.

Irregularity, for contracting marriage while bound by religious vows, 120-123.

Independent Order of Good Templars, 62.

Infamy.

Irregularity, as above.

Jurisdiction, impeding exercise of, 56.

laymen capable of, 102, 103.

Katipunan Society, 61.

Ku-Klux Klan, 61.

Knights of Pythias, 62.

Knights Templars, 62.

Legates of the Holy See, 52.

Legitimate civil power, 62.

*Liber Sextus* of Boniface VIII, 18, 19.

Machinate, against church or state, 62.

Mandates, of Pope, Legate, Bishop, 52.

Marriage—attempted by religious with solemn vows, 111ff.

attempted or contracted by religious of simple vows, 117ff.

Masons and Masonic sects, 59ff.

Novitiate, admission to, 132ff.

Office, see below.

Ordinary, Proper, 51 footnote.

excommunication reserved to, for apostasy from religion, 98.

for marriage or attempted marriage by religious of simple vows, 117.

is to punish delinquents for neglect of diocesan conferences, 82.

Commercial trading, 84.

violation of common life, 124.

spending dowries, 144.

neglect to notify him of approaching reception or profession, 146.

interference with liberty of conscience, 149ff.

Office, privation of:

for conspiracy or inciting to disobedience against Pope, Legate or Proper Ordinary, 53.

for passing laws against rights of church or hindering exercise of ecclesiastical jurisdiction, 58.

for joining Masonic and similar sects, 60.

for violation of cloister by admitting women therein, 66.

for forgery of apostolic documents, 79.

as fugitives, 101.

for violation of common life, 124.

for admitting unfit subjects to novitiate and profession, 138.

for interference with canonical visitation, 142.

for spending dowries, 144.

for failure to notify ordinary of

approaching reception or profession, 148.

for interfering with freedom of Sisters' confessions, 152, 153.

Suspensions: of fugitives, 101.

of major superior who sends subjects to alien Bishop for ordination, 129-131.

Voice, Active and Passive, privation of: for conspiracy against Pope, Legate, Ordinary, 53.

for passing laws against rights of Church or hindering exercise of ecclesiastical jurisdiction, 58.

for joining Masonic and similar sects, 60.

for admitting or introducing women into cloister, 66.

for forgery of documents of the Holy See, 79.

as a fugitive, 101.

for violation of common life, 124.

# CANON LAW STUDIES

1. FRERIKS, REV. CELESTINE A., C.PP.S., J.C.D., Religious Congregations in Their External Relations, 121 pp., 1916.
2. GALLIHER, REV. DANIEL M., O.P., J.C.D., Canonical Elections, 117 pp., 1917.
3. BORKOWSKI, REV. AURELIUS L., O.F.M. De Confraternitatibus Ecclesiasticis, 136 pp., 1918.
4. CASTILLO, REV. CAYO, J.C.D., Disertacion Historico-canonica sobre la Potestad del Cabildo en Sede Vacante o Impedida del Vicario Capitular, 99 pp., 1919 (1918).
5. KUBELBECK, REV. WILLIAM J., S.T.B., J.C.D., The Sacred Penitentiaria and Its Relations to Faculties of Ordinaries and Priests, 129 pp., 1918.
6. PETROVITS, REV. JOSEPH, J. C., S.T.D., J.C.D., The New Church Law on Matrimony, X-461 pp., 1919.
7. HICKEY, REV. JOHN J., S.T.B., J.C.D., Irregularities and Simple Impediments in the New Code of Canon Law, 100 pp., 1920.
8. KLEKOTKA, REV. PETER J., S.T.B., J.C.D., Diocesan Consultors, 179 pp., 1920.
9. WANNENMACHER, REV. FRANCIS, J.C.D., The Evidence in Ecclesiastical Procedure Affecting the Marriage Bond, 1920.  (Not Printed.)
10. GOLDEN, REV. HENRY FRANCIS, J.C.D., Parochial Benefices in the New Code, IV-119 pp.,  (Printed 1925.)
11. KOUDELKA, REV. CHARLES, J., J.C.D., Pastors, Their Rights and Duties According to the New Code of Canon Law, 211 pp., 1921.
12. MELO, REV. ANTONIUS, O.F.M., J.C.D., De Exemptione Regularium, X-188 pp., 1921.
13. SCHAAF, REV. VALENTINE THEODORE, O.F.M., S.T.D., J.C.D., The Cloister X-180 pp., 1921.
14. BURKE, REV. THOMAS JOSEPH, S.T.B., J.C.D., Competence in Ecclesiastical Tribunals, IV-117 pp., 1922.
15. LEECH, REV. GEORGE LEO, J.C.D., A Comparative Study of the Constitution "Apostolicae Sedis" and the "Codex Juris Canonici," 179 pp., 1922.
16. MOTRY, REV. HUBERT LOUIS, S.T.D., J.C.D., Diocesan Faculties According to the Code of Canon Law, II-167 pp., 1922.
17. MURPHY, REV. GEORGE LAWRENCE, J.C.D., Delinquencies and Penalties in the Administration and the Reception of the Sacraments, IV-121 pp., 1923.
18. O'REILLY, REV. JOHN ANTHONY, S.T.B., J.C.D., Ecclesiastical Sepultuae in the New Code of Canon Law, II-129 pp., 1923.
19. MICHALICKA, REV. WENCESLAS CYRILL, O.S.B., J.C.D., Judicial Procedure in Dismissal of Clerical Exempt Religious, 107 pp., 1923.

20. DARGIN, REV. EDWARD VINCENT, S.T.B., J.C.D., Reserved Cases According to the Code of Canon Law, IV-103 pp., 1924.
21. GODFREY, REV. JOHN A., S.T.B., J.C.D., The Right of Patronage According to the Code of Canon Law, 153 pp., 1924.
22. HAGEDORN, REV. FRANCIS EDWARD, J.C.D., General Legislation on Indulgences, II-154 pp., 1924.
23. KING, REV. JAMES IGNATIUS, J.C.D., The Administration of the Sacraments to Dying Non-Catholics, V-141 pp., 1924.
24. WINSLOW, REV. FRANCIS JOSEPH, A.F.M., J.C.D., Vicars and Prefects Apostolic, IV-149 pp., 1924.
25. CORREA, REV. JOSE SERVELION, S.T.L., J.C.D., La Potestad Legislativa de la Iglesia Católica, IV-127 pp., 1925.
26. DUGAN, REV. HENRY FRANCIS, M.A., J.C.D., The Judiciary Department of the Diocesan Curia, 87 pp., 1925.
27. KELLER, REV. CHARLES FREDERICK, S.T.D., J.C.D., Mass Stipends, 167 pp., 1925.
28. PASCHANG, REV. JOHN LINUS, J.C.D., The Sacramentals According to the Code of Canon Law, 129 pp., 1925.
29. PIONTEK, REV. CYRILLUS, O.F.M., S.T.B., J.C.D., De Indulto Exclaustrationis necnon Saecularizationis, XIII-289 pp., 1925.
30. KEARNEY, REV. RICHARD JOSEPH, S.T.B., J.C.D., Sponsors at Baptism According to the Code of Canon Law, IV-127 pp., 1925.
31. BARTLETT, REV. CHESTER JOSEPH, A.M., LL.B., J.C.D., The Tenure of Parochial Property in the United States of America, V-108 pp., 1926.
32. KILKER, REV. ADRIAN JEROME, J.C.D., Extreme Unction, V-425 pp., 1926
33. McCORMICK, REV. ROBERT EMMETT, J.C.D., Confessors of Religious, VIII-266 pp., 1926.
34. MILLER, REV. NEWTON THOMAS, J.C.D., Founded Masses According to the Code of Canon Law, VII-93 pp., 1926.
35. ROELKER, REV. EDWARD G., S.T.D., J.C.D., Principles of Privilege According to the Code of Canon Law, XI-166 pp., 1926.
36. BAKALARCZYK, REV. RICHARDUS, M.I.C., J.U.D., De Novitiatu, VIII-208 pp., 1927.
37. PIZZUTI, REV. LAWRENCE, O.F.M., J.U.L., De Parochis Religiosis, 1927. (Not Printed.)
38. BLILEY, REV. NICHOLAS MARTIN, O.S.B., J.C.D., Altars According to the Code of Canon Law, XIX-132 pp., 1927.
39. BROWN, BRENDAN FRANCIS, A.B., LL.M., J.U.D., The Canonical Juristic Personality with Special Reference to its Status in the United States of America, V-212 pp., 1927.
40. CAVANAUGH, REV. WILLIAM THOMAS, C.P., J.U.D., The Reservation of the Blessed Sacrament, VIII-101 pp., 1927.
41. DOHENY, REV. WILLIAM J., C.S.C., A.B., J.U.D., Church Property: Modes of Acquisition, X-118, pp., 1927.

42. FELDHAUS, REV. ALOYSIUS H., C.PP.S., J.C.D., Oratories, IX-141 pp., 1927

43. KELLY, REV. JAMES PATRICK, A.B., J.C.D., The Jurisdiction of the Simple Confessor, X-208 pp., 1927.

44. NEUBERGER, REV. NICHOLAS J., J.C.D., Canon 6 or the Relation of the Codex Juris Canonici to the Preceding Legislation, V-95 pp., 1927.

45. O'KEEFFE, REV. GERALD MICHAEL, J.C.D., Matrimonial Dispensations, Powers of Bishops, Priests, and Confessors, VIII-232 pp., 1927.

46. QUIGLEY, REV. JOSEPH, A.M., A.B., J.C.D., Condemned Societies, 139 pp., 1927.

47. ZAPLOTNIK, REV. IOANNES LEO, J.C.D., De Vicariis Foraneis, X-142 pp., 1927.

48. DUSKIE, REV. JOHN ALOYSIUS, A.B., J.C.D., The Canonical Status of the Orientals in the United States, VIII-196 pp., 1928.

49. HYLAND, REV. FRANCIS EDWARD, J.C.D., Excommunication, Its Nature, Historical Development and Effects, VIII-181 pp., 1928.

50. REINMANN, REV. GERALD JOSEPH, O.M.C., J.C.D., The Third Order Secular of Saint Francis, 201 pp., 1928.

51. SCHENK, REV. FRANCIS J., J.C.D., The Matrimonial Impediments of Mixed Religion and Disparity of Cult, XVI-318 pp., 1929.

52. COADY, REV. JOHN JOSEPH, S.T.D., J.U.D., A.M., The Appointment of Pastors, VIII-150 pp., 1929.

53. KAY, REV. THOMAS HENRY, J.C.D., Competence in Matrimonial Procedure, VIII-164 pp., 1929.

54. TURNER, REV. SIDNEY JOSEPH, C.P., J.U.D., The Vow of Poverty, XLIX-217 pp., 1929.

55. KEARNEY, REV. RAYMOND A., A.B., S.T.D., J.C.D., The Principles of Delegation, VII-149 pp., 1929.

56. CONRAN, REV. EDWARD JAMES, A.B., J.C.D., The Interdict, V-163 pp., 1930.

57. O'NEIL, REV. WILLIAM H., J.C.D., Papal Rescripts of Favor, VII-218 pp., 1930.

58. BASTNAGEL, REV. CLEMENT VINCENT, J.U.D., The Appointment of Parochial Adjutants and Assistants, XV-257 pp., 1930.

59. FERRY, REV. WILLIAM A., A.B., J.C.D., Stole Fees, X-107 pp., 1930.

60. COSTELLO, REV. JOHN MICHAEL, A.B., J.C.D., Domicile and Quasi-Domicile, VII-201 pp., 1930.

61. KREMER, REV. MICHAEL NICHOLAS, A.B., S.T.B., J.C.D., Church Support in the United States, VI-136 pp., 1930.

62. ANGULO, REV. LUIS, C.M., J.C.D., Legislación de la Iglesia sobre la intención en la applicación de la Santa Misa, VII-104 pp., 1931.

63. FREY, REV. WOLFGANG NORBERT, O.S.B., A.B., J.C.D., The Act of Religious Profession, VIII-174 pp., 1931.

64. ROBERTS, REV. JAMES BRENDAN, A.B., J.C.D., The Banns of Marriage, XIV-140 pp., 1931.

65. RYDER, REV. RAYMOND ALOYSIUS, A.B., J.C.D., Simony, IX-151 pp., 1931.

66. Campagna, Rev. Angelo, Ph.D., J.U.D., Il Vicario Generale del Vescovo, VII-205 pp., 1931.

67. Cox, Rev. Joseph Godfrey, A.B., J.C.D., The Administration of Seminaries, VI-124 pp., 1931.

68. Gregory, Rev. Donald J., J.U.D., The Pauline Privilege, XV-165 pp., 1931.

60. Donohue, Rev. John F., J.C.D., The Impediment of Crime, VIII-110 pp., 1931.

70. Dooley, Rev. Eugene A., O.M.I., J.C.D., Church Law on Sacred Relics, IX-143 pp., 1931.

71. Orth, Rev. Clement Raymond, O.M.C., J.C.D., The Approbation of Religious Institutes, 171 pp., 1931.

72. Pernicone, Rev. Joseph M., A.B., J.C.D., The Ecclesiastical Prohibition of Books, XII-267 pp., 1932.

73. Clinton, Rev. Connell, A.B., J.C.D., The Paschal Precept, IX-108 pp., 1932.

74. Donnelly, Rev. Francis B., A.M., S.T.L., J.C.D., The Diocesan Synod, VIII-125 pp., 1932.

75. Torrente, Rev. Camilo, C.M.F., J.C.D., Las Processiones Sagradas, V-145 pp., 1932.

76. Murphy, Rev. Edwin J., C.PP.S., J.C.D., Suspension Ex Informata Conscientia, XI-122 pp., 1932.

77. MacKenzie, Rev. Eric F., A.M., S.T.L., J.C.D., The Delict of Heresy in its Commission, Penalization, Absolution, VII-124 pp., 1932.

78. Lyons, Rev. Avitus E., S.T.B., J.C.D., The Collegiate Tribunal of First Instance, XI-147 pp., 1932.

79. Connolly, Rev. Thomas A., J.C.D., Appeals, XI-195 pp., 1932.

80. Sangmeister, Rev. Joseph V., A.B., J.C.D., Force and Fear as Precluding Matrimonial Consent, V-211 pp., 1932.

81. Jaeger, Rev. Leo A., A.B., J.C.D., The Administration of Vacant and Quasi-Vacant Episcopal Sees in the United States, IX-229 pp., 1932.

82. Rimlinger, Rev. Herbert T., J.C.D., Error Invalidating Matrimonial Consent, VII-79 pp., 1932.

83. Barrett, Rev. John D. M., S.S., J.C.D., Comparative Study of the Third Plenary Council and the Code, IX-221 pp., 1932.

84. Carberry, Rev. John J., Ph.D., S.T.D., J.C.D., The Juridical Form of Marriage, X-177 pp., 1934.

85. Dolan, Rev. John L., A.B., J.C.D., The Defensor Vinculi, XII-157 pp., 1934.

86. Hannan, Rev. Jerome D., A.M., S.T.D., LL.B., J.C.D., The Cannon Law of Wills, VI-517 pp., 1934.

87. Lemieux, Rev. Lelisle A., A.M., J.C.D., The Sentence in Ecclesiastical Proceduce, IX-131 pp., 1934.

88. O'Rourke, Rev. James J., A.B., J.C.D., Parish Registers, IX-109 pp., 1934.

89. TIMLIN, REV. BARTHOLOMEW, O.F.M., A.M., J.C.D., Conditional Matrimonial Consent, X-381 pp., 1934.

90. WAHL, REV. FRANCIS X., A.B., J.C.D., The Matrimonial Impediments of Consanguinity and Affinity, VI-125 pp., 1934.

91. WHITE, REV. ROBERT J., A.B., LL.B., S.T.B., J.C.D., Canonical Ante-Nuptial Promise and the Civil Law, VI-152 pp., 1934.

92. HERRERA, REV. ANTHONY PARRA, O.C.D., J.C.L., Legislacion Ecclesiastica sobre el Ayuno y la Abstinencia, 1935.

93. REILLY, REV. PETER, J.C.L., Residence of Pastors, 1935.
Cases of Evident Nullity, 1935.

94. MANNING, REV. JOHN J., A.B., J.C.L., Presumption of Law in Matrimonial Procedure, 1935.

95. MOEDER, REV. JOHN M., J.C.L., The Proper Bishop for Ordination and Dimissorial Letters, 1935.

96. O'MARA, REV. WILLIAM A., Canonical Causes for Matrimonial Dispensations, 1935.

97. REILLY, REV. PETER, J.C.L., Residence of Pastors, 1935.

98. SMITH, REV. MARINER T., O.P., S.T.Lr., J.C.L., The Penal Law for Religious, 1935.

99. WHALEN, REV. DONALD W., A.M., J.C.L., The Value of Testimonial Evidence in Matrimonial Procedure, 1935.

CPSIA information can be obtained at www.ICGtesting.com
Printed in the USA
BVOW05*0501010415

394166BV00001B/1/P